Curriculum workshop

Routledge Education Books

Advisory editor: John Eggleston
Professor of Education
University of Keele

Curriculum workshop
An introduction to whole curriculum planning

Maurice Holt

Routledge & Kegan Paul
London, Boston, Melbourne and Henley

First published in 1983
by Routledge & Kegan Paul plc
39 Store Street, London WC1E 7DD,
9 Park Street, Boston, Mass. 02108, USA,
464 St Kilda Road, Melbourne,
Victoria 3004, Australia, and
Broadway House, Newtown Road,
Henley-on-Thames, Oxon RG9 1EN
Set in Times 10 on 11 pt
Printed in Great Britain by
T. J. Press (Padstow) Ltd
Padstow, Cornwall
© Maurice Holt 1983

Library of Congress Cataloging in Publication Data

Holt, Maurice.

Curriculum workshop.
(Routledge education books)
Bibliography: p.
Includes index.
1. Curriculum planning—Great Britain—Case studies.
I. Title.   II. Series.
LB1564.G7H64   1983   375'.001'0941   83–10918

ISBN 0–7100–9512–0 (pbk.)

Contents

Contents

Preface

This book aims to help schools with the business of whole curriculum planning. It arises from my experience as head of a comprehensive school which began a common curriculum for all its pupils in 1969, and successfully continues to do so; from my subsequent work as an independent curriculum consultant; and, most recently, from the programmes I have arranged at a college of higher education for school-based in-service courses and the professional development of teachers.

The book is intended both for teachers – whether newly appointed, in middle management, or heads – and for all those concerned with the governance and administration of schools. It takes into account the string of national documents on the curriculum which have followed in the wake of the 1977 Green Paper *Education in Schools* from the Department of Education and Science. In particular, it is a response to the Department's Circular 6 of 1981, *The School Curriculum*, which states that local education authorities, governing bodies, heads and the staff of schools 'should work towards the common end of securing a planned and coherent curriculum within the schools'.

The tasks of reviewing and planning the curriculum are not, however, easy ones to undertake. In schools, they imply a dimension of professionalism which has not been encouraged in the past. And they presuppose a degree of detailed knowledge about education and curriculum on the part of governing bodies, and a concern among LEA advisers and administrators for a view of the curriculum as something more than a timetable setting out a collection of subjects.

This book hopes to be of value not by presenting set solutions, nor by offering an account of the various pieces of educational theory which bear upon the problems of curriculum planning. It offers not so much answers, but ways of getting to answers. It gives importance to the need to identify curriculum problems, and have a defensible method for solving them.

Every school will generate its own agenda of problems – of curriculum tasks which require solution. If the resulting solutions are to be justified, a prerequisite is that those who are deliberating about the curriculum are aware of the context within which the curriculum is to be determined. The first chapter is therefore concerned to set the scene; to summarise recent documents and reports, and indicate criteria by which they might be judged.

Chapter 2 is concerned with the next step: with the approach to curriculum planning, and the considerations which arise when the issues of curriculum design, control and assessment are tackled. Some current concerns are discussed, and there is a simulation exercise which has been found useful in preparing teachers and others for the business of curriculum design.

Finally, Chapter 3 presents a number of case studies of secondary schools which have embarked on whole curriculum planning, and an account of responses in two primary schools to the issues raised by recent national documents. Each case study serves as a source of ideas, and of questions: by reflecting on practical solutions which have been found to work, one can gain an understanding of the constraints and conflicts within which solutions must be found, and of the kind of reasoning which is likely to lead to the best solution.

The book attempts to cover a considerable amount of ground in a small compass, and to prepare the reader for discussion of issues which invariably lead to judgments of value. As a result, alternative points of view are in places presented more briefly than I would like. By the same token, I have not attempted to adopt a neutral stance: this seems untenable and unworkable. Instead, by making my own views plain, I hope they may more readily be challenged, and lead to reflection and discussion on the points at issue.

At critical points in the book, the reader is invited to consider particular topics which arise; and although extensive reference to other sources has been avoided in the text, these are listed at the end of the book and should be useful to those seeking further information. Altogether, the exercises, case studies and summaries should be of value to a school, a study group or an individual engaged in the arts of whole curriculum planning.

The title of this book is intended to say something about how I think it might best be used: as a source of ideas to discuss, argue about and deliberate upon. It is not a book which propounds some idealised design and develops it to a final result by the application of fixed principles. On the contrary, it argues that to look for such principles is to misconceive the nature of curriculum process. Instead, it is about the 'workshop' activity of getting one's bearings by looking at curriculum documents, of practical exercises to clear the ground, and then of looking at examples of practice and thus nourishing the process of deliberation.

In arguing that curriculum problems cannot be solved by the procedural application of formal principles, however, I am not for a moment suggesting that a curriculum can be constructed without reasoned discourse and informed method. Moreover, I argue that a curriculum must reflect a rationale of education and society, and that this rationale must govern the essentially moral process by which curriculum building takes place. It is my belief that only by leaving behind the futile search for technocratic procedures, and concentrating on the practical interpretation of curriculum problems, can we give real weight to these moral issues and see curriculum design and implementation as a single whole. I hope the book will help its users – it is meant to be used, as well as read – to make this vital link between theory and practice.

Acknowledgments

A book of this kind incorporates ideas from a number of sources and I am grateful to all the teachers with whom I have discussed curriculum planning: many of their contributions have influenced the following pages. I owe a particular debt to Bill Reid, senior lecturer in Education at the University of Birmingham, whose insight into curriculum issues has been most helpful and stimulating. I am grateful, too, to Mike Golby, senior lecturer in Education at the University of Exeter. I have found our discussions over some years of the greatest value, and he was kind enough to comment on the first draft of the book. So also was my colleague Douglas Ireland, of the College of St Mark and St John: to him, and to my other colleagues David Gorbutt and Paul Rolph, go my thanks for many helpful curriculum sessions. I am grateful to Tony Parfitt, deputy head of Eggbuckland School, Plymouth, for reading the first draft and making many useful comments on it.

I am much indebted to the headteachers of the schools discussed in Chapter 3, who were kind enough not only to let me visit their institutions, but also to allow me to write about them and to correct the errors in my account. I should like to extend my personal thanks to David Payne (Berkeley Vale School, Gloucestershire); Peter Cornall (former headmaster of Carisbrooke School, Isle of Wight – now Senior Inspector of Schools for Cornwall); David Grubb (Gillott's School, Henley-on-Thames, Oxfordshire); Malcolm Woodward (Holsworthy School, Devon); Keith Greenwood (Kingshill School, Cirencester, Gloucestershire); Arthur Spencer (Priory School, Weston-super-Mare, Avon); Gertrude Seddon (Sheredes School, Hoddesdon, Hertfordshire); Jean Halton (Bassett's Farm Primary School, Exmouth, Devon); and Graham Rowland (former headmaster of Woodbury Primary School – now of Feniton Primary School, Devon).

The extracts from government publications referred to in Chapter 1 are reproduced with the permission of the Controller of Her Majesty's Stationery Office. The extract from *Core Curriculum for Australian Schools* in Chapter 2 is reproduced with the kind permission of Professor Malcolm Skilbeck of the University of London Institute of Education, and of the Curriculum Development Centre, Canberra.

Chapter 1

Problems and prescriptions: the curriculum context

In a number of schools, headteachers, staff and governors have begun to consider questions like these:

Does the curriculum give adequate weight for all pupils to 'performance' subjects like art, music and drama?
Are the specialist skills of the staff effectively deployed, so that all pupils have access to them?
How does the proportion of resources devoted to the teaching of option groups relate to that devoted to the core curriculum?
Is the curriculum broad, balanced and coherent for all pupils?

It is no longer taken for granted that the curriculum of primary or secondary schools is a matter to be left to the professionals, whether they be teachers or curriculum developers; and the professionals themselves no longer assume that the curriculum as it is must represent the best that can be done. It is recognised that the school curriculum expresses educational policy, and that what a pupil takes away from school is a matter of curriculum decisions.

The curriculum, in short, will attract increasing attention from press, public and the profession. Teachers will be required to justify curriculum decisions, both to themselves and to lay observers. These decisions will not get easier, as the world becomes more complex and uncertain. New technology will change the nature of work and leisure, and our views of education itself will change in response to new patterns in society.

This current of doubt and inquiry will be felt in other professions. Doctors, for example, may now find their judgment of a patient's condition challenged in the courts. Just as the concept of education is under review, so also is the concept of health. But the work of teachers is much closer to the parent, politician and

1

industrialist than that of the doctor. The immediate results of teaching are instantly visible in the home and in the classroom. And there seems to be no limit to the tasks society places on the schools; social, political, health and moral education are all seen as matters for the school curriculum to tackle, at a time when the traditional family unit can no longer be taken for granted, and when we recognise that schools must also respond to the multi-cultural community in which we all live.

The nature of curriculum problems

The professional role of the teacher will, therefore, have to extend to take account of these pressures. In a word, we must recognise that what teachers do is *solve curriculum problems*.[1] All the questions listed above define curriculum problems. Here are some more:

1 What shall I teach 3L on Monday morning?
2 Should we use file paper or exercise books in first year history?
3 Ought we to spend the science capitation on more circuit boards for the third years, or start introducing new textbooks?
4 Should we drop the lunchtime computer club, and spend the time planning a new O level option in computer studies?
5 Is there a case for linking art and craft in a new five-year design course for all pupils?
6 Is it right to exclude pupils from the school during morning break and after lunch?

The conventional view of teacher professionalism assumes that most of these questions are matters for the head of department, or even the headteacher. The first question has to be solved all the time, and yet it is no less important than the others. And to the able, aware teacher, the answer is never obvious. It is not simply a matter of content; content and method are interlinked, and the answer must take account of the resources available, the pupils themselves, and the broad aims of the particular department as well as of the school.

The second question may seem a private matter for the first year history staff. But pupils will go on to the second year, and filed work might be a good basis for what is to follow. So the history department as a whole ought to examine the matter. But perhaps there is a proposal to link history and geography in the first two or three years. In that case, the geographers ought to be brought in.

In any event, which is cheaper? Is next year's capitation likely to run to the provision of a file for every pupil? It would be wise to talk to the co-ordinator for resources, or to the deputy head with this responsibility.

In the same way, the fourth question turns out not to be a private issue for the mathematics staff. The computer club means that all interested pupils can get access to computing. If it becomes an examination option, only those who can fit it into their choices – and who have the requisite ability – can do it. And where will the teaching time come from to staff the option? In any case, is computing merely to do with mathematics?

The next question clearly raises the matter of co-operation between the art and craft departments, and possibly home economics and fabric as well. So it points towards discussion on a faculty basis. But it also raises a fundamental question to do with the whole curriculum: is there a case for requiring all pupils to engage in a design course, from 11 to 16? Does this represent worthwhile curriculum experience for everyone?

The last question looks, at first sight, like one for the head to resolve. But if pupils are free to go in and out of the school during breaks, they will need to be supervised. Are the staff prepared to do this at lunchtime? What are the supposed benefits? Will the pupils be better off? Will their morale be enhanced, but at the price of an additional load on staff?

None of these problems, it turns out, has an obvious answer. Yet they will not go away. Some action is called for: they are *practical* problems to which some sort of answer must be found.[2] By contrast, much educational research is devoted to the pursuit of *theoretical* problems, which we may or may not find interesting. For example, the problem of why a particular form of pupil grouping gives better results than another may appeal to the university researcher, who may eventually write a paper about it and then leave it for good. His work may, possibly, be of interest to teachers in due course – perhaps even of some value. But the practical problems faced all day long by teachers are of a quite different, and infinitely more urgent, nature from the theoretical problems pursued by most academics.

Moreover, practical curriculum problems are not capable of solution by following a set of rules: we cannot determine the right solution by some ineluctable sequence of instructions. If the overhead projector won't work, we can adopt a *procedural* solution to find the answer; we can check the fuse, the plug, the bulb and so on. But if a teacher finds a particular mathematics

3

exercise has been badly done, there is no prescription which will tell him why this is; he can only look again at the work and its context, reflect upon his intentions and actions, perhaps discuss the matter with his colleagues, and then arrive at a defensible course of action. And, at the end of the day, this course of action may not produce the desired effect: curriculum problems are both practical and *uncertain*.

There is a further important characteristic of the uncertain, practical problems which underline curriculum action. They are also *moral* problems. In solving them, we must consider not merely our own good, but rather the good of the pupils whom we ultimately serve. It may, for example, be more convenient to teachers if pupils use file paper, since it is easier to carry around a bundle of papers to mark for homework than a pile of exercise books. Buying more science apparatus may make the task of setting up the lessons easier. Running O level computer studies will look good when a teacher applies for another job. Keeping craft as a separate department makes life easier. Turning pupils out at lunchtime guarantees a quiet half hour for everyone in the staff room. But, in practice, teachers respond as professionals to a recognition that the education of their pupils gives them a moral responsibility.

There is, of course, nothing new about this part of the job. But what is new is the recognition that the job cannot be isolated within one's own particular classroom, or one's own subject boundary. The decisions that must be taken transcend these boundaries. So every teacher is not just a teacher of some subject; he is professionally part of the whole curriculum of the school. How has this enlargement of professionalism come about?

The cause is simply the fact that society requires all pupils to be offered not any old education, but a good education; and a good education can no longer be seen as a more or less haphazard collection of subjects. A good education has to prepare every pupil for the business of living, in a world where adaptability and personal qualities are as important as specialist knowledge. If, as adults, they will need to look at the world in a coherent and balanced way, then as pupils they will need a curriculum which takes a coherent and balanced view of our culture.

For the moment, the interpretation of coherence and balance will not be taken further. But already this relatively mild observation has challenged the kind of secondary curriculum on offer in the schools studied in the HMI secondary survey *Aspects of Secondary Education* (1979). The survey shows that an emphasis on separate subjects pursued for their own sake, and on free choice between subjects in option systems, has led to incoherence and imbalance. Already we are in conflict with the grammar school model of the curriculum which our secondary schools inherited from the nineteenth-century public schools.

Once we begin to challenge received practice by identifying curriculum problems – by recognising that the curriculum is problematic – we need ways of handling these problems and seeing them as a characteristic of school activity. Hence the value of the classification outlined above. Solving them then becomes a matter of *practical reasoning* – which is built up by reflection upon actions and the way they can be justified. It owes much to common sense, but it is more than that: it is to do with fostering a professional tradition by looking at practice in a critical way, generating new insights and trying out fresh possibilities. In this deliberative way, we transcend common sense to create knowledge about practice. Theory and practice inform each other.[3]

On this critical view, the reorganisation of secondary education into comprehensive schools is not a matter of political doctrine, but merely an acknowledgment of the need to provide for all pupils a common curriculum in common schools. The challenge of living a full and happy life in a complicated industrial society means that it is not enough to offer this pupil an education that is good for university entrance, that pupil one that is good for the building site round the corner; all pupils need an education that is, in its own terms, good.

We are therefore confronting the task of establishing a comprehensive curriculum; and it is something which schools have not in general begun to do. And it clearly is a matter which involves not only judgments about the organisation of learning and the contributions of subjects: it also must take account of a school's constituency, and of the national context. So it is not really so surprising that the school curriculum has become a major focus of attention.[4]

Curriculum planning in perspective

Yet it amounts to a significant shift of emphasis from the climate within which, until recently, schools operated. Until 1976 curriculum questions were seen chiefly as matters best left to schools themselves. In the post-war years a low priority was generally given to whole curriculum issues. During the 1950s, the need was to build new schools to meet the demands of the baby boom. In the 1960s, growing affluence and a mood of release from austerity led to comprehensive schools and less rigid teaching in primary schools. But few questions were asked about what the curriculum should be; appropriate forms of organisation were seen as of prior importance. This is not a new phenomenon: the 1944 Norwood Report said little about the curriculum of its proposed secondary modern schools.

The tendency is illustrated by the Department of Education and Science Circular 10 of 1965, requiring local education authorities to go comprehensive. The document makes no mention of what might be an appropriate curriculum; it is concerned to list the kinds of scheme – of rearrangements of buildings – which would be acceptable. Similarly, the adoption of middle schools in some areas for pupils aged 8–13 or so came about not because the educational virtues of these schools had been demonstrated, but because they were a technically convenient way of distributing pupils between the educational plant available.

Even so, schools were free – within the confines of the examination system – to pose curriculum problems and devise solutions. For the 1944 Education Act released secondary schools from a nationally controlled curriculum; the last Regulations for Secondary Schools had appeared in 1935. And the Elementary Regulations for what were now to become primary schools had been abolished in 1926.

Yet secondary schools, at any rate, were slow to seize this chance to work out better forms of curriculum, probably because the curriculum was not recognised as the crucial educational element. For the 1950s and most of the 1960s, the debate was dominated by the research of sociologists and psychologists on selection and the 11-plus examination, and equality of opportunity was seen as a matter of providing the right facilities and forms of organisation rather than the right curriculum. Conventional curriculum patterns went unchallenged.

Two events of 1964 will illustrate this. First, the Certificate of Secondary Education was launched – a new examination aimed not at the top 20 per cent of the ability range, like Ordinary Level (O level) of the General Certificate of Education, but at the next 40 per cent below. Thus a new form of assessment now existed for 60 per cent of the ability range in any given subject, but the binary examination system precisely mirrored the bipartite structure of secondary education – of grammar schools and secondary modern schools. The dual curriculum was not challenged, and neither was the idea of treating the curriculum as the sum of separate subjects. Instead, the new examination was a further boost to both assumptions, since few schools took up the opportunity of devising their own examinations, and those that did rarely established new subject mixes.

The other event of 1964 was the establishment of the Schools Council for Curriculum and Examinations. Nuffield science projects were already under way, and substantial curriculum development had begun in the USA. But although the council became quite quickly the prime agency in the UK for curriculum development, its projects were mainly conceived in subject terms, and again mainly reflected the bipartite curriculum structure. Thus geography for the young school leaver was aimed at the average and below average pupil: geography 14–18 for the above average. And for every project like that based at Keele for integrated humanities,[5] there were many more in conventional subjects.

All this changed in the 1970s. For one thing, the school leaving age was raised in 1973, and the number of pupils in comprehensive schools had increased tenfold in the ten years since 1965. Britain was at last in the business of mass secondary education from 11 to 16, but without an appropriate curriculum for the task. Another factor was the 1973 oil crisis, coming on top of economic difficulties and early signs of a wider recession. As a big spender, education suddenly became a vulnerable industry. Most important, perhaps, was a change of mood; the optimism and hope of the 1960s had given way to doubt and talk of accountability. Since 1969, right-wing critics of what they saw as soft-centred progressivism had called for a return to traditional standards. This 'back-to-basics' movement had begun even earlier across the Atlantic. With hindsight, we can perhaps identify the 1967 Plowden Report on Primary Education as the final romantic flowering of post-war optimism. Thereafter it was to be uphill work for those looking forward to new ideas rather than backward to old ones.

As criticism of schools mounted in the tabloid press, political action became likely. In 1974 the Prime Minister of the incoming Labour administration, Mr Callaghan, asked the Education Secretary (Mr Mulley) for a report on the state of schools. In 1975 this was circulated confidentially within the DES as the 'Yellow Book'. It made stringent criticisms of schools, but perhaps its most significant statement was a positive one: that a common curriculum should be adopted for secondary schools. The conversion of Her Majesty's Inspectorate and of the DES civil servants to this notion marked a radical departure, since it pointed irrevocably towards the need to view the curriculum as a whole, and not – as on the grammar school model – as a range of subjects chosen according to personal whim for the most part.[6]

We may pinpoint 1976 as the critical year in post-war curriculum planning, since that autumn Mr Callaghan, speaking at Ruskin College, Oxford, drew heavily on the Yellow Book in calling for a 'great debate' on education. The new Education Secretary (Mrs Williams) established a series of set-piece 'debates'[7] around the country, and in the following year the 1977 Green Paper was published. This purported to reflect the preceding 'debate', but in essence adopted the agenda and the opinions of the Yellow Book. The Green Paper declared the intention of the DES to inquire into the local authorities' arrangements for the school curriculum, and to investigate the idea of establishing a 'framework for the curriculum'. In due course these documents appeared, as also did a number of reports from HMI on curriculum issues. Whereas, during the 1960s, HMI had made a virtue of taking a back seat, the policy was now to go into print and declare a view.

Finally, in March 1981, the DES published *The School Curriculum*, offering 'guidance to the local education authorities and schools in England and Wales on how the school curriculum can be further improved'. And with the publication in October 1981 of Circular 6, the circle was completed; the Secretary of State now 'looks to governors to encourage their schools, within the resources available, to develop their curricula, in the light of what is said in "The School Curriculum"'. Thus, in the five years since the Ruskin speech in October 1976, the DES has reasserted its former influence over the curriculum.

To argue, however, that the DES seeks central control is to overstate its enthusiasm for handling curriculum issues and its financial resources. Equally, it is naive to suppose that civil servants are locked into a conspiracy to subvert the pattern of schooling and replace it with a system of their own choice. The muddle and misunderstanding which are attendant on hierarchical bureaucracies like the HMI and DES would soon put paid to any formalised plot. What is, however, true is that senior civil servants hold in common some assumptions about society and their part in it. A few in key positions have great influence, and their shared understandings – mainly implicit – about social philosophy have allowed the DES not only to sustain a single point of view through several changes of government, but also to move from opposite prompt to centre stage in a short space of time. The DES exhibits nothing so coherent and explicit – and therefore assailable – as a *policy*: rather – which is infinitely more persistent, yet elusive – a set of implicit, shared *beliefs*.

The purpose of this introduction is to set the scene for the tasks of curriculum planning called for in *The School Curriculum*, and with which this book is concerned. But as well as sketching in the historical background, I hope it also shows that there is an inevitability about these recent events. By clinging to the bipartite, grammar school model of curriculum, the schools and – regrettably – the Schools Council had left a policy vacuum which the DES was, by 1975, ready to fill. And, just as the Board of Education in its 1904 Regulations set out the form of that grammar school curriculum, so the DES in 1981 set out the lineaments of a comprehensive curriculum.

The remainder of this chapter presents a summary of the key DES and HMI documents, so that the reader can establish exactly what conclusions have been reached about the present pattern of schooling, and exactly what new directions are indicated. But it is not the intention that these diagnoses and prescriptions should be adopted uncritically. The comments offered in the course of these summaries indicate debatable questions and unresolved issues, and some of these will be taken further in later chapters.

Curriculum design: recent national interventions

Since the publication of the Green Paper *Education in Schools* in 1977, seven documents on the curriculum have been published by the DES which are of particular importance; four of these stem from HMI, and three from the DES secretariat. They are:

1 *Curriculum 11–16* (1977), HMI;
2 *Primary Education in England* (1978), HMI;
3 *Local Authority Arrangements for the School Curriculum* (1979), DES;
4 *Aspects of Secondary Education* (1979), HMI;
5 *A Framework for the School Curriculum* (1980), DES;
6 *A View of the Curriculum* (1980), HMI;
7 *The School Curriculum* (1981), DES.

The character of these documents is different: each serves a particular political or administrative purpose and stands on its own. But, taken together, they amount to an indictment of the present curriculum in primary and secondary schools, and a manifesto for a new curriculum.[8]

All are significant, but some much more so than others for our purpose, which is to examine pointers to whole curriculum planning. For the primary curriculum, documents 2 (the primary curriculum survey), 6 and 7 are the key ones. For the secondary curriculum, document 1 develops themes which are taken up later in the sequence; the secondary survey (4) is both descriptive and prescriptive; while documents 6 and 7 again give a curriculum overview.

1   Curriculum 11–16 (1977)

This is usually known as 'the Red Book'. The foreword states that this collection of papers 'have been overtaken by events. . . . They are working papers written by a group of HMI for discussion by HMI. . . . They take their place along with all the other writings about the curriculum'.

The Official Secrets Act prevents us from knowing how the HMI and DES officials go about their business.[9] We can only guess that the Red Book began as a working party of HMI in the early 1970s, before reshaping the secondary curriculum became a political fact.[10] Although dated 1977, a printers' strike delayed publication until 1978. By this time the Green Paper had appeared, but we can assume that the key papers in the Red Book were circulating within the DES at least by 1975, when the secret Yellow Book was being written. Thus although the Red Book was 'overtaken by events', it is at least arguable that it influenced DES policy at a critical stage. For one thing, the Yellow Book embraces the idea of a common curriculum; the Red Book's first section is entitled 'The Case for a Common Curriculum in Secondary Education to 16'. For another thing, the DES Assessment of Performance Unit officially began work in 1975, and its approach to the task of evaluating the curriculum is set out in a paper 'Monitoring school performance', written by the HMI in charge of the APU. This paper was published in the DES house journal *Trends in Education* in July 1975, and its six 'lines of development' for the curriculum bear a striking resemblance to the Red Book's eight 'areas of experience'.[11]

In the following summary, the words and figures used are those of the original documents. My own comment or clarification is in brackets throughout.

Page

3 The hierarchical organisation of many secondary schools
does not give the majority of teachers the sense and
experience of being involved in fundamental educational
thinking . . . [Curriculum decisions, in other words, have
been seen as matters for the chiefs, rather than the Indians.
This is consistent with a subject-based, fragmented,
grammar-school model.]

3 . . . A major obstacle to coherent development is the sense
of 'autonomy' of the individual school . . . and a deep
reluctance to face the implications of partnership in
curriculum planning. [School and teacher autonomy are
seen as barriers to change. The 'partnership' model argues
for closer links between schools, LEAs and HMI.]

5 We believe there are general goals appropriate for all
pupils, which have to be translated into curricular
objectives in terms of subjects/disciplines/areas of learning
activity. If . . . more agreement could be reached
nationally about these objectives, then the consequences of
the diversity of schemes of secondary reorganisation . . .
could be mitigated. . , . . There is a lot to be said for all
those concerned with the drawing up and teaching of
curricula defining their aims and objectives . . . [An
important passage, making three points which reappear in
later documents. First, that education implies 'general
goals' – i.e. some form of common curriculum – for all
pupils; second, that these need to be formulated at
national, not local, level; and third, that the goals can be
turned into curriculum experience by the procedures of
stating aims and defining objectives.]

5 Pupils are members of a complicated civilisation and
culture, and it is reasonable to argue that they have nothing
less than a right to be introduced to a selection of its
essential elements.[12] [Curriculum is seen as a selection from
the culture;[13] and access to it is seen as a right for all
pupils.]

5 Option systems may well prevent this from happening; the
freedom to stop studying history, or art, or music, or
biology at 14 means that pupils are not being given the
introduction to their own cultural inheritance . . . [An
explicit attack on option systems in years 4 and 5,[14] which
were almost universally adopted by comprehensive schools

during the 1960s and 1970s: and the implication that to give pupils their curriculum birthright means restricting freedom to choose between subjects.]

6 We see the curriculum to be concerned with introducing pupils during the years of compulsory schooling to certain essential 'areas of experience'. . . . It is a checklist . . . for curricular analysis and construction. . . . None of the areas listed should be simply equated with a subject or group of subjects. . . . Subject or 'course' labels often tell us surprisingly little about the objectives to be pursued. . . . It is not proposed that schools should plan and construct a common curriculum in terms of subject labels only. . . . It is necessary to look through the subject or discipline to the areas of experience and knowledge to which it may provide access . . .

6,7 *Checklist*

Example of compulsory curriculum:

Areas of experience	*Subject*	*Periods*
The aesthetic and creative	English	5
The ethical	Mathematics	5
The linguistic	A modern language	4
The mathematical	A science	5
The physical	RE and a social study	4
The scientific	Art/Craft/Music	4
The social and political	Careers education	2
The spiritual	Physical activities	3

The list . . . does not in itself constitute an actual curricular programme . . . . What are of prime importance are the intentions and learning objectives to be realised, and the coherence and balance of the total programme for each pupil.

It is based on a 40-period week and corresponds to our estimate that the common curriculum should occupy two thirds or more of the total time available. . . . Such curriculum construction in terms of subjects is acceptable . . . only when everyone is clear about what is to be achieved through them.

[This section forms the crux of the argument. The curriculum must have 'coherence' and 'balance': terms to be repeated in later documents. The eight 'areas of experience' should be compared with the APU's six 'lines of development': aesthetic, ethical, verbal, mathematical, physical, scientific. The APU was later to subsume the remaining areas of experience under the 'ethical', and re-christen it 'personal and social development'. The eight areas are seen not as a curriculum programme in itself, but as ways of interpreting subject contributions. Subjects are seen not as ends in themselves, but as means to further ends framed by the eight areas.]

9 The educational system is charged by society . . . with equipping young people to take their place as citizens and workers in adult life . . . [But there is also] the responsibility for educating the 'autonomous citizen' . . . these two functions do not always fit easily together. [The first responsibility dominates Mr Callaghan's Ruskin speech: 'To equip children . . . for a lively, constructive place in society and also to fit them for a job of work'. Is this the responsibility of training, and the second that of education?]

11 Society can demand that schools are places in which pupils and teachers work hard . . . and in which certain qualities and attitudes . . . are established, by example as well as by precept. [Accountability is linked with the puritan work ethic, for staff and pupils. But is it less 'hard work' if a teacher spends less time in class contact, and more time planning? Are MPs slacking when they are absent from the chamber? This passage reflects the late 1970s mood that schools should give 'value for money'.]

12 Schools must, therefore, be capable of adopting methods suitable to different needs; objectives will have been stated clearly, methods must be flexible to achieve them. [Again, great faith is placed in the precise statement of objectives[15] in implementing curriculum intentions.]

Summary
Curriculum 11–16 is an admirably bold document of uneven quality, but which is sympathetic to the way schools work and which hits some important targets. It makes a case for a radical departure from the traditional 'core plus option' system, towards a high-level, 'big-core' programme which sees subjects as means to more elaborate curriculum ends. It has had considerable influence on later documents. But it has some serious deficiencies:

1 Arguing for a common curriculum in terms of pupils' rights has drawbacks. Why should not pupils have a right to free driving

lessons? There is talk of the curriculum as a selection from the culture; but this means little without a clearer understanding of the criteria for selection.[16]

2   The same absence of any rationale for education is evident when the 'areas of experience' suddenly appear. Where do they come from? What do they mean? (Later, a sheet of further definitions was produced; but the problem of meaning remains.) They appear to be a decoction of Hirst's 'forms of knowledge and understanding', set out first in 1965.[17] But these result from a carefully argued logical analysis and incorporate an explicit view of what constitutes educational experience. Without such explication, it is difficult to see the areas of experience as much more than gestures in the direction of a broader curriculum. Moreover, Hirst's interpretation of liberal education – upon which his forms rest – is one not shared by others.[18]

3   Again, without some theory of education to inform the argument, it is difficult to see what 'balance' and 'coherence' mean. Balance between what alternatives? Coherence according to what general principle? What proportion of time spent on each area of experience constitutes 'balance'? Is there some connection between 'coherence' and subject integration?[19]

4   There is a strong emphasis on writing down 'clear objectives'. There is a belief running through the document that once aims and objectives are established to everyone's satisfaction, the right curriculum will follow. This is to assume that curriculum problems are procedural; and also that means and ends can be separated in curriculum activity. There is much to suggest that, on the contrary, means and ends are interacting and that the least important part of the curriculum is what can be written down.[20] It may be that the curriculum, like the British constitution, is best seen not as a set of principles, objectives and procedures but rather as a platform of shared values and understandings. (This point will be taken further in Chapter 2.) In this case, the Red Book is weak where it needs to be strong: on explaining just what educational values inform its judgments.

5   While the document takes a step in the right direction in arguing for a high-level common curriculum, it falters when one begins to consider how such a programme might be implemented. The political dimension of curriculum change is entirely omitted; so also is any understanding of how teachers

might approach new curriculum tasks. If we try to determine how far this is a matter for national intervention, how far a question of 'partnership' or how far a task for the autonomous school, we find the document confused. The notion of school-based curriculum development is absent – indeed, school autonomy comes in for criticism. But how, in the last analysis, is the curriculum actually going to change?

2   *Primary Education in England (1978)*

The HMI primary survey is a short, closely written document which need not be dissected in detail. Instead, the reader is urged to look at the document itself and at some commentaries on it.[21] What follows is an outline of the principal points made in the survey, and a summary of the criticisms which might be made of it.

The survey differs from earlier reports on primary education, and most markedly from the Plowden Report, published eleven years earlier. It does not set its study in a historical perspective; its language is more prescriptive; it does not assume that by and large, English primary education is there to be admired. It is not content to rely on mere description; it uses systematic observation and, in part, quantitative measurement; it is centred not so much on a model of the child's growth and experience, as on a view of liberal education and the kinds of learnings which should therefore be fostered.

In particular, it is a critical survey and offers no grounds for complacency. It states quite firmly that, as far as low-level 'basic skills' are concerned, primary teachers give them priority. Reading test scores are reassuring, in 90 per cent of classes there is a quiet working atmosphere, and in 19 classes out of 20, children are given adequate guidance about their work. Significantly, though, it was found that performance on basic skills was best in schools which saw them as part of a broad curriculum.

The curriculum is a major focus: while Plowden devotes only 12 per cent of its space to curriculum issues, they occupy two-thirds of the survey. Teaching styles and classroom organisation give way to the problems of determining necessary skills and knowledge and how to incorporate them. It is found that science, craft, history and geography are largely neglected. It is suggested that responsibility allowances might with advantage be given to teachers so as to extend specialist influence, and that all teachers should be more aware of whole curriculum issues: traditionally, these have been left to the head, while the individual teacher is free to organise his or her programme idiosyncratically. It was found, however, that in less than a third of classes were pupils undertaking work in all the curricular items listed as desirable by the HMI, who concluded that 'ways of providing a more consistent coverage for important aspects of the curriculum need to be examined'.

Another major focus was the extent to which the work undertaken by children matched their capacity to do it. This was examined in each curriculum area, for the most able, average and least able as identified by their teachers. It was found that the most able fared worst, the least able best: the ablest were not sufficiently challenged, especially in inner city schools.

The survey found that in three-fifths of classes, children have little opportunity to use books from choice or for pleasure, and that children rarely took part in observational or experimental work. Techniques in mathematics were rarely used in everyday settings.

Summary
The survey gives a picture of primary schools as being worthy places, but perhaps rather dull. It finds a strong emphasis on the basics, evidently at the expense of a broader curriculum. There is not much evidence that primary schools are alive with creative activity, with pupils embarking on voyages of personal discovery and teachers acting as guides and facilitators. One is led to wonder whether the Plowden revolution ever actually occurred; or whether, if it did, it has all changed. A 1981 survey[22] compares the aims of primary teachers in 1971 and 1979, and finds that in 1979 teachers put less emphasis on creativity, self-control and developing a questioning attitude, and on courtesy and good social mixing. Instead, mathematics, spelling and grammar are seen as of most importance.

A 1980 research study[23] used systematic classroom observation to examine life in primary classrooms. It found that pupils were kept very busy on some task or other; that heavy weighting was given to basic skills; and that children spent most of their time working on their own rather than interacting with others. Group work was used as a way of organising pupils rather than a teaching strategy in its own right.

These findings are generally consistent with the HMI survey. Primary classrooms are hives of industry, particularly where basic skills are concerned. But the range of experiences may not be very broad, or very deep: the more able are not sufficiently stretched, and topic work (especially in geography and history) may be isolated bits rather than a sustained programme. Pupils are beavering away on their own, without perhaps being provoked to observe sharply, to discuss freely, to look critically at the world around them. There is little trace of Plowdenism to be seen.

What needs to be questioned, however, is whether the changes sought by the primary survey are going to improve matters. Some specific weaknesses can be characterised:

1 The way the report went about its task is an indication of the attitudes it favours. The survey adopts a product model of the curriculum: it is to be measured by its results.[24] In each of the survey schools two classes were assessed by HMI, heads and teachers completed questionnaires and NFER tests in reading and mathematics attainment were applied. This is a managerial approach, leaning heavily on assessment techniques which may be subject to stringent criticism.[25] Using these data the important conclusions on 'matching' were developed; but it might be argued that the data should take account of process rather than product. Similarly, the suggestion that responsibility should be delegated for particular curriculum areas applies a secondary school model to what might be an inappropriate setting. It is a managerial solution, but one which begs important questions about the purpose of primary education.

2 The survey is subject-centred rather than child-centred. Yet the survey uncovers little evidence of genuine child-centred activity (and the other research studies confirm this). So the merits or demerits of child-centredness – of a developmental approach – cannot really be pronounced upon.[26] The survey chooses to disregard this historical tradition in favour of an externalised, subject-centred approach. This may be a good thing; but we cannot assume that it will be. Structures and posts of responsibility are important only in so far as they support the imaginative response of teachers to the intellectual task of solving curriculum problems in the classroom.[27] The report throws little light on this.

3 In particular, it is by no means clear how the greater intellectual development of pupils advocated by the report is to be secured. In places a greater range of subjects is advocated: but merely increasing the load of science content is not going to enhance intellectual activity. Again, it looks as if secondary school practice is being urged upon primary schools without

17

adequate reflection. There is also a disturbing emphasis on the idea of *skills* as aspects of general intellectual development.[28] In science, for example, 'it is essential that children should develop observational skills'. But are 'observational skills' of this generalised nature? Can they be intellectualised in this way? Are such skills not associated with particular contexts? If so, this emphasis on skills is wholly misleading and directs us to a cul de sac, when we should be looking at other curriculum issues.

In summary, the importance of the primary survey in considering the range of DES documents 1977–81 is its clear indication that schools should be judged on output measures of performance. Curriculum change is to be output-led – in line with other technocratic developments like the APU – and not input-led, as implied by Plowden's concern to judge schools in the round and promote 'genuine virtues' like 'neatness, accuracy and persistence'. Managerial devices like posts of responsibility are to be used to ensure that an externalised model of curriculum is firmly implanted. The articulating force in the curriculum will be a set of desired ends rather than the perceptions of the class teacher. Mr Chips has finally given way to Mr Checklist. What is significant is not the survey's proposals in themselves – some of which have much to commend them – but the way in which they are handled and the implicit production model of schooling. This is a feature, to a greater or lesser extent, of all the official documents.

3   Local Authority Arrangements for the School Curriculum (1979)

DES Circular 14 of 1977 invited local authorities to answer a series of questions about their arrangements for resourcing, assessing and controlling the curriculums of their schools. The Circular was seen as a centralist intrusion by some teachers' organisations, and it was no secret that many of the replies were viewed by their authors as works closer to fiction than fact. But the Circular stemmed directly from the 1977 Green Paper, and its underlying assumption was entirely consistent with the view that schools could not be trusted to make their own decisions. Yet in some LEAs (notably Hertfordshire) the idea of even collecting data from schools about their curriculums had been seen as anathema, and as a rejection of the policy that schools work best when given

autonomy and encouragement and responsible heads and governors. Circular 14/77 takes the opposite view: schools work best
when their policies are centrally orchestrated. And it assumes that
LEAs are competent to carry out this kind of monitorial control.
The ambivalence of many LEA officers towards the Circular
reflects their doubts about this assumption: not because this kind
of administrative control is especially difficult, but because it may
not be worth doing. The supposed gain in accountability may be
offset by the loss in educational quality.

The report on the answers to Circular 14/77 is, like most
non-books, a collection of miscellaneous items. The key part of
the document is the brief commentary at the beginning, from
which the following extracts are taken:

Page

2   Local authorities' policies . . . should not stand in isolation.
    They must be seen in the context of the relationships
    between all the parties with responsibilities for school
    education: central and local government, school governing
    bodies and teachers. The Secretaries of State do not intend
    to alter the existing statutory relationship between these
    various partners. [This is a firm espousal of the
    'partnership' model.]

2   Nevertheless the Education Acts lay upon Ministers the
    duty to 'promote the education of the people of England
    and Wales'. . . . The Secretaries of State do not seek to
    determine in detail what the schools should teach or how it
    should be taught; but they have an inescapable duty to
    satisfy themselves that the work of the schools matches
    national needs. [Here is a shift of emphasis from
    partnership towards accountability. Essentially, what is
    being urged is a diminished role for the partners; they are
    needed, but only inasmuch as they reinforce central
    policies. Some partners are more equal than others. That
    way, the 'top-down' model can be made to work.][29]

3   Authorities [should not] seek a detailed control of school
    curricula in their areas; but [they have] a responsibility to
    formulate curricular policies and objectives which meet
    national policies and objectives and command local
    assent. . . . The formulation of local policies . . . would be
    improved if local authorities were better informed about
    the curricular practices and aims of their schools and the
    extent to which the schools are successful in achieving these

aims. [It is assumed that national policies will 'command local assent'; this need not be the case. Yet LEAs are now in the business of curriculum policy-making, and of curriculum evaluation. But this is another contentious matter.]

3 . . . Curricular matters are often in practice devolved [by the governors] upon the head teacher and staff. Whatever the formal responsibilities of governing bodies there should always be the closest consultation and co-operation between the governors, head teacher and staff. [This sounds like a warning shot across the bows of the professionals; 'co-operation' sounds sensible enough, but governing bodies are political institutions, and can change their affiliations. What happens then to consistent, coherent curriculum policies?]

4 A nationally agreed framework for the curriculum is obviously very significant for teacher policies and resources. . . . Many authorities need to increase their working knowledge of what goes on in their schools, in order to improve their capability to develop and implement more effective approaches to staffing, curriculum development, assessment and the distribution of resources . . . [This is conventional line management doctrine: but it may be that education is an alien field in which to apply it. In any case, such approaches to management are now out of favour with industry.[30] The tendency is to decentralise and give more autonomy to individual, self-accounting organisations – of which schools are a ready-made form.]

6 The Secretaries of State . . . believe they should seek to give a lead in the process of reaching a national consensus on a desirable framework for the curriculum . . . [Devising the framework becomes a task for the centre, to be reached by 'consensus'.]

Summary

This document shows clearly the consistency of intentions in the DES, regardless of the government of the day. For Circular 14/77 was the work of a Labour Secretary (Mrs Williams), and its assumptions were warmly endorsed in the subsequent report by a Conservative Secretary (Mr Carlisle). It was a foregone conclusion that the report would establish what everyone knew; that LEAs had not troubled to acquire a detailed knowledge of school curriculum policies, least of all attempted the forlorn task of evaluating schools. The Circular was a device which managed to make the LEAs look as if they were failing in their duties, and thus allowed the DES to take the initiative.

4 Aspects of Secondary Education (1979)

What follows is a brief abstract of facts and figures (and of some opinions) from the HMI secondary survey. It complements the official summary of the survey, which gives its general conclusions chapter by chapter. Both are a poor substitute for the report itself, which contains much valuable analysis. My intention here is to draw attention to those observations which throw light on current curriculum practice, and on the case for whole curriculum planning in particular.

Page

2   The survey concentrated on the final two years of compulsory schooling. [A school's policy for fourth and fifth year pupils is perhaps the best quick guide to its curriculum policy and its educational thinking.]

4   The survey was planned as a series of inspections covering a 10 per cent sample of maintained secondary schools . . . directed towards four aspects of education: . . . language skills, mathematical understanding and competence, scientific skills and understanding, and the personal and social development of the pupils.

7   [Only 42 per cent of the 384 schools studied were full-range comprehensives – FRCs henceforth – although 54 per cent were termed comprehensive. On average – p.10 – comprehensives had about 1000 pupils, and only 7 per cent of them had over 1600 pupils. The notion that comprehensives are very large rarely applies.]

9   [Of all the schools, 63 per cent had sixth forms; 82 per cent made curricular provision for 11–16 pupils; 78 per cent of all comprehensives provided for 11–16 pupils; 86 per cent of all comprehensives were mixed.]

14   The policy of the majority of schools is to keep the curriculum as broad as possible in the first, second and third years. . . . Only 11 per cent of the schools stated that they offered a wholly common curriculum in the first three years. . . . The majority indicated . . . differentiation . . .

21

according to . . . sex and ability . . . [Whatever the intention, pupils in the first three years are offered a variety of curricular programmes.]

15 Differentiation by sex in the craft subjects [in the first three years] occurred . . . in something over 65 per cent of the schools. [Only in 48 per cent of FRCs was there a wholly open choice of craft subjects.]

16 [Less than 3 per cent of the FRCs used a full-range mixed-ability organisation in the third year. There was subject setting in two-thirds of the schools, increasing from years 1 to 3. The notion that comprehensives widely adopt mixed-ability grouping has little foundation in fact.]

17 By the fourth year [remedial teaching] had virtually disappeared. [In FRCs third year setting was more common in English than in foreign languages. Comprehensives are more inclined than grammar schools to set in English and science. It appears that subject setting is well entrenched in comprehensives.]

19 [Two-thirds of the responding schools made the second foreign language in the third year alternative to another subject – usually a craft subject, or geography occasionally.] The price paid . . . is the loss or severe reduction of contact with the creative/aesthetic area of the curriculum [art, music and the crafts] for the able pupils concerned.

20 [All but four schools allowed second foreign languages and separate science subjects in the fourth year only to those pupils who had taken them when available in the second and third years. In effect, key decisions restricting curricular choice were therefore widely made as early as the second year. Also, pupils rarely took, in years 4 and 5, subjects they had been obliged to drop earlier – for example, craft subjects dropped by abler pupils.]

21 In nearly 20 per cent of the schools curricular choices were made without the benefit of advice from specialist careers teachers about the possible effects of such choices.

The Fourth Year Curriculum
[In 31 per cent of the FRCs, the common core was differentiated by ability bands.]

22 [On average, 42 per cent of the timetable in FRCs was devoted to the core. Maths and English were always found,

with PE also in 90 per cent of schools. In FRCs, 51 per cent offered RE in the core; 22 per cent did not.]

23   As with religious education, the pupils for whom [careers education] was not provided tended to be those of higher ability. [A form, house or tutor period was added in about 20 per cent of schools; a music period in 8 per cent.]

25   Pupils were generally required to select between 4 and 6 subjects from the total available [in the option columns] . . . 4 or 5 periods were allocated to each of these optional subjects. [How do schools determine 4 or 5 periods as the allocation? This can make a big difference to the range offered under the option scheme – a whole option block.]

26   The average number of between 19 and 24 separate subject or course titles [offered in the option scheme] may be regarded as large. [Note – p.226 – that comprehensive schools offered on average 37 examination subjects.] Grammar schools . . . were more likely to provide a large number of academic subjects . . . and . . . reduce their provision in the creative and aesthetic area of the curriculum. . . . School size . . . seemed to have little effect on the number of optional subjects. . . . There was no clear relationship between the number of additional languages offered and the presence or absence of a sixth form, or its size. [This supports the case for 11–16 schools, with a break at 16.]

27   Variations both in the level of staffing and in the qualifications of teachers . . . were extremely wide.

29   [Uncertainty about the meaning of curriculum balance: in some schools this meant including all areas of the curriculum in each pupil's programme, but in others the essential subjects were those thought to have vocational importance or significance for higher education, which were then 'balanced' by subjects from a different area of the curriculum. And in 23 per cent of the FRCs, the options were offered in 2 or 3 bands – not necessarily along with a banded core.]

29   [With banded options, the lower bands had more practical subjects and fewer sciences.] In a number of schools with an apparently open options systems some pupils were, in effect, banded because of the restrictions placed upon their choice. . . . The option system could and often did permit programmes differentiated not by ability but by sex . . .

30 [Sometimes the lowest band was supplied with a 'packaged' course, with large time allocations to 'environmental studies', 'integrated humanities', 'design for living' and so on. In about 20 per cent of the grammar schools, 'express streams' were to be found. Such programmes for the most able pupils had similar features: they stressed academic and examination subjects at the expense of a wider general education, with no careers education and sometimes no RE.]

31 One period of European studies, one of 'humanities' and one of art . . . did not seem likely to be of great benefit. . . . Subjects or courses also obviously intended for the less able pupils could often be found in option blocks . . . it was difficult to avoid the conclusion that they, too, were timetable fillers.

In general . . . schools spend much time and effort . . . in devising arrangements of great complexity to permit the maximum amount of pupil choice . . .

The Fifth Year Curriculum

32 [In 80 per cent of schools with a common core, teachers were used in option subjects at 1.3 to 1.6 times the rate in core subjects. In half the schools, core subjects were taught in forms of entry, yet most six form-entry schools offered nine or ten subjects in the option blocks.]

33 [The average class size for optional subjects was below twenty in more than two-thirds of the schools. Groups of less than twelve pupils tended to occur in additional languages and in music.]

34 [In English, four pupils out of five were taking GCE or CSE. 15 per cent of the classes were bigger than 30 pupils.]

35 [In French, roughly three girls take it to every two boys. In FRCs, an average of 32 per cent of fourth year pupils took French. The rest had dropped it.] Schools respond to the many demands made on them by parents, pupils and society at large by extending the range and number of the subjects they offer. This, they believe, also improves pupils' motivation. . . . Less able pupils are given in effect less real choice than other pupils.

38 The prospect of being able to drop some subjects may constitute a disincentive to sustained effort well before the stage of choice is reached. . . . Too often pupils simply stop three-fifths of the way through a five-year course, without

much consideration being given to the nature of the experience and the value of the attainment. . . . Allowing substantial numbers of pupils to drop subjects at 14 has other implications. . . . Science . . . history and geography give particular cause for concern.

39 There are limits to the number of subjects in which setting is likely to be practicable . . . There may also be some limits on how much setting is desirable, given that an organisation . . . could result in the pupils working in differently composed groups for every subject . . . The curricular programmes of the more able were markedly similar in both grammar and full range comprehensive schools.

39 Schools more commonly expected intending scientists to devote 4 [sometimes 5] periods a week to each of the three separate sciences. Yet 8, rather than 12 or more periods out of the 40 would seem to be a satisfactory proportion . . . for this area of the curriculum. . . . The system commonly resulted in abler pupils having to choose at 14 or earlier between science and languages . . . or . . . both at the expense of the humanities and the creative-aesthetic areas of the curriculum . . .

42 Teachers need a view of the school curriculum as a whole and the part they are playing in it if they are to co-ordinate their pupils' learning and provide them with some sense of coherence in their programmes. . . . Specialist teachers naturally want to teach their subject to the highest level. . . . But if these subjects are to contribute more effectively to the broad education of the pupils many specialist teachers will have to break away from the isolation in which they commonly work.

43 Subjects can be interpreted in appropriate ways to meet identified needs [like careers, health and political education] but only if the subject specialists have consulted and planned together . . . Organisation has grown increasingly complex and it is surely time to think about a somewhat simpler structure. . . . The process has been one of aggregation rather than a revaluation of changing circumstances accompanying the growth of comprehensive education . . . Schools have been subject to increasing, sometimes conflicting, pressures and many of them have responded as best they can within a framework which itself calls for reconsideration.

Staffing

45 [Nearly 50 per cent of teachers in FRCs were graduates. In all schools, only 5 per cent have BEd degrees. Just over half the heads of departments in all schools were graduates. In FRCs, one-third of all the teachers had more than ten years' teaching experience.]

51 Further investigation . . . indicated a hierarchy of grammar, full range comprehensive, restricted range comprehensive and modern schools, both in the subject match and the levels of qualification of the teachers. The shortages of teachers with appropriate subject qualifications often occurred in subjects in which there is particular public interest: religious education, English, mathematics and science.

52 [41 per cent of remedial teachers did remedial teaching only. A high proportion were part time, and 35 per cent had less than five years' experience. Of exclusively remedial teachers, only 15 per cent had a qualification in maths or science. Of English teachers, 22 per cent had no qualification in English. In FRCs, 19 per cent of RE teachers had none.]

54 Many heads of English departments necessarily confined their own teaching to the examination years and the sixth form.

55 [Almost two-thirds of French teachers were women, and 10 per cent part-time.]

58 Even within schools of the same type and size and catering for the same age range there were very marked variations [in the level of staffing. For example, two schools both had 1400 pupils with 190 in the sixth form. One was staffed at 1:11.1, the other at 1:19.1. About one-third of teachers held special responsibility allowances for curriculum posts, and a further 10 per cent for pastoral care.]

59 [The average pupil-teacher ratio for schools of about 1000 pupils is about 17.0. For FRCs, the average contact ratio is 0.78. But there are wide variations between schools of the same type and size, reflecting different kinds of compromise between more time for non-teaching functions, and the desire to provide a range of curricular choice.]

61 [The average additional non-teaching time set aside for heads of departments was less than two periods; for those with a major pastoral role, between four and five periods.]

63 The distribution of staff shows more generous use for the older year groups, particularly the fourth and fifth years where it is devoted mainly to the option systems . . . [Staff to run the options are used at the expense of the lower school, as the table on p.62 shows clearly for two sample schools.]

64 The presence or absence of a sixth form makes no significant difference to the operational pupil-teacher ratios in any of the first five years. [There was very wide variation in pupil-teacher ratio for the same years among schools of the same type. In FRCs, first years varied from 16.0 to 22.0; second years from 17.0 to 21.8.]

65 The claim that schools are over-managed and that teachers are spending too much time on duties other than teaching was not supported by the evidence of the survey.

Language

73 Whatever enthusiasm for reading might have been developed in the earlier years, the survey revealed a narrowing in the scope and quality of reading by most fourth and fifth year pupils. . . . In at least a quarter of the schools it was the less able who suffered particularly from a failure to extend their reading or to provide an appropriate range of material.

76 Where whole-class teaching in streams or sets prevailed, the reading of the more able or average might be a single textbook. [Setting does not, therefore, seem to benefit either the more able or the less able. A topic approach may be helpful.] It was refreshing to find 'comprehension' material . . . being used to illuminate . . . some central text or topic.

79 There was no recorded instance of a 'remedial' specialist working alongside a subject specialist in the classroom. [Further evidence of curriculum fragmentation, and the remoteness of much remedial work.] Many fourth and fifth year pupils are doing little reading of any kind.

82 In recent years the pressure of external examinations has affected more and more pupils.

85 [Note-taking dominates.] Good memories, a logical turn of mind, quick verbal facilities and strong motivation made the process smooth enough, but the stimulation that able pupils need to extend their language was lacking.

27

95 In the quarter of schools in which drama lessons were observed, the emphasis was mainly on the production of plays and the study of play texts. [The value of drama as a curriculum subject may be little exploited.]

102 About 10 per cent of all the schools were in areas of considerable social deprivation. [A relatively low proportion.]

102 The policies for language across the curriculum . . . recommended by the Bullock Report are difficult to achieve. . . . It may be, indeed, that the phrase itself . . . is not forceful enough to convey the notion of the overall responsibility of all teachers for the development of language.

106 A precipitate attempt to write the 'policy' called for by the Bullock recommendations had resulted only in undermining the professional confidence of staff . . . [Important implications for the nature of whole-curriculum change: exhortations to devise 'policies' may have little impact.] It was, disappointingly, often true that some energetic LEA initiatives . . . had not succeeded sufficiently in priming the pump in the schools themselves. [In what ways can advisers be most effective? Are other support services needed?]

107 A change of emphasis from language as evidence of learning achieved to language used in the process of learning is needed. [This shift of emphasis from the product to the process has wider implications for curriculum planning.]

Mathematics

162 In some cases good leadership from the head of department produced teaching of a quality dramatically greater than that to be found in schools which were comparable in all other respects. . . . In most schools a measure of external support [with in-service training] is to be recommended. [The key role of the head of department, and the need to provide in-service training for him or her, is a recurring theme.]

Science

164 Schools offered a wide range of science courses. [Only 12 per cent of schools required pupils to take at least one science in years 4 and 5.] 9 per cent of the boys and 17 per

cent of the girls did no science in their fourth and fifth years, and about 50 per cent and 60 per cent respectively were studying only one science subject.

166 There is more biology studied than either physics or chemistry . . .

168 Large numbers of girls as well as boys do not follow balanced science courses in years 4 and 5 . . . girls do substantially less science than boys in these years. . . . Girls are much more likely to select biological sciences and boys to select physical sciences.

176 [In over 40 per cent of the schools, there was fewer than one full-time technician to four laboratories, which was considered inadequate.]

180 [About one in five physics teachers has no qualification in physics.]

183 In about one-third of all the schools the teaching of science was always or nearly always overdirected, with insufficient pupil activity.

184 Few opportunities were provided for pupils to conduct challenging experimental investigations. . . . Only 25 per cent of the schools visited appeared to make sensible and regular use of demonstrations. [Nuffield may have over-stressed the place of class practical work.]

185 In about one-third of all schools it was apparent that insufficient demands were made of able pupils.

188 In many schools, the acquisition of knowledge was the main feature of the science courses; only rarely was the emphasis on teaching the process of science rather than the subject matter. [Again, a fundamental curriculum issue.]

190 More opportunities could with advantage be given to pupils . . . to pit their wits against a problem and advance their own plans for its solution.

192 In about one-third of the schools visited the dominant teaching style was exposition from the teacher with little or no pupil involvement . . .

196 In roughly 10 per cent of the schools, some of the pupils in the fourth and fifth years were provided with a balanced science curriculum. . . . No school was found, however, which provided balanced science courses for all pupils up to the age of 16-plus. . . . Examples were found of pupils getting a narrow experience of science . . . by opting for, say, 'applied electricity' or 'human biology' as their only science subject. . . . There is a strong case for offering to all

pupils up to the age of 16-plus balanced science courses embracing the basic elements of physics, chemistry and biology at depths and with teaching approaches appropriate to their ability.

197 Balanced science courses may be of more value to the pupils if they are presented in a unified way.

198 There is much to be said for science teachers regarding themselves . . . as science educators. . . . Experience of existing 'double-subject' broad science courses at O level seems to indicate that they can provide an adequate preparation for A level science courses. . . . If science courses were provided for all pupils up to the age of 16, up to 20 per cent more science teachers would be required . . . [But this assumes double-subject science provision for all in years 4 and 5: for some, a single-subject unified course might be appropriate.]

204 Good results had more to do with the teachers themselves than with the teaching material. [A comment on the impact of Nuffield, which seems to have little correlation with pupil performance.]

205 [Only 3 per cent of the FRCs were doing SCISP; 86 per cent were making little or no use of the project.]

Personal and Social Development

209 Analysis . . . showed that the 13 to 18 comprehensive schools were markedly less successful than 11 or 12 to 18 full range comprehensive schools in providing for the personal development of their pupils. . . . Many [schools] need to go further in establishing a clear policy agreed by head and staff which can be translated in the organisation of subjects, the content of individual subjects and the teaching and learning methods used. . . . Such an overall view of the curriculum is rare.

210 There did not seem to be any greater overall planning of the curriculum in the [13 per cent of] schools that had set up faculty structures: in many of these schools faculties seemed to be more concerned with general organisational matters than with curriculum planning. . . . There were schools . . . of all types in which there was little evidence of substantial staff discussion about the school curriculum as a whole. [Faculties have often been introduced purely to facilitate timetabling and organisation, without a corresponding attempt at curriculum planning.]

212 In the 11 per cent of schools which were making notably good provision for their pupils' development . . . the pastoral system was closely linked to the academic structure of the school. Once established, the relationships in these schools seemed to have become self-generating . . . [Hence, perhaps, the importance of appropriate means for *initiating* curriculum change.] The over-use of highly prescriptive worksheets was noted in many schools.

218 Some schools . . . showed that they could be successful in relating the demands of external examinations to more general educational objectives. . . . Examinations were not ignored but they were not given more than their due weight.

219 The survey showed that over three times as many schools of all types employed year systems rather than house systems . . .

220 In small schools it is clear that the care of the individual was possible without complex organisational structures.

223 About a third of the schools . . . were very well led. . . . Most heads in these schools initiated ideas and policy, but also readily encouraged ideas in others and reconciled opposing interests and views.

228 The most successful guidance practices observed were those in which the balance and appropriateness of a pupil's curriculum was the concern not only of the . . . tutor . . . and the head of year or house but also of the various subject specialists.

229 In-service training has an important part to play in helping schools to develop both the skills of individuals and teamwork within the institution. [Hitherto, the emphasis has mainly been on the former. Developing the latter will require fresh initiatives.]

232 In general the potential for careers education within the subjects of the curriculum was not being exploited.

236 [37 per cent of the schools provided work experience for their fifth year pupils.] In many schools only a small proportion of the year group was involved [in work experience] and these were usually of average or below average ability.

238 One-sixth [of the schools] were assessed very favourably [in respect of personal and social development]. . . . There were on the other hand an equal number of schools where the provision . . . was assessed as unsatisfactory. . . .

Schools place great emphasis on fostering their pupils' development by means of pastoral structures and organisations. Much would be gained if equal emphasis was placed on the learning in the classroom and the teaching of an appropriate curriculum. [This last observation is unusually outspoken, but justified by the survey's results.]

239 The teachers often blamed the pressures of external examinations for limitations in the secondary curriculum . . . There is evidence, however, that confident and assured teachers, particularly if supported by the local community, are able to meet the requirements of external examinations without harmful effects on the curriculum and teaching styles. [An important reference to the need for a strong community base to a school's curriculum plan.]

Public Examinations

244 In practice . . . the majority of these [Mode 3 examination] courses are intended for pupils of average ability and below . . .

245 In 80 per cent of the cases the LEA forbade or discouraged double entry [for examinations].

246 The lower [O level] grades D and E were said to carry more prestige with many parents and employers than the possibility of a grade 1 at CSE. . . . The decision to enter a pupil . . . for a particular type of examination may also be the product not of educational but of organisational considerations. [Banding systems may be the determinant.]

247 About one third of the schools were making unrealistic demands on some pupils, with too high expectations of some and under expectations of others. . . . Too many pupils were allowed to opt out of examinations in some schools.

248 When Mode 3 examinations were the outcome of coherent courses they were said to have a liberating effect. [The virtues of well-planned Mode 3 courses are thus acknowledged, and not just for lower-ability pupils.] Rightly or wrongly, examination results were commonly perceived by the school as the sole indicator of its success in the eyes of the community . . . there is a passive acceptance of the system and the pressures it imposes on the schools.

249 Pupils and their parents have a right to expect not only examination success but also that schools should promote valuable personal and intellectual qualities such as

curiosity, the ability to express views orally, the capacity to work as a member of a team and to work independently.

General

266 The evidence of this survey is that many pupils are not well served by the curricular structures and organisations of their schools. . . . The complex organisation of teaching groups, which in large part derives directly from the complex option systems, often makes it difficult for teachers themselves to make connections or to help their pupils to do so.

267 Both educational needs . . . and practical considerations argue for some re-examination of the assumptions which underlie the prevailing pattern of curricular provision. In particular the evidence of this survey suggests a need for all pupils to carry forward a broader programme of studies to the end of . . . compulsory education, with a corresponding reduction in the number of 'options' taken . . . and a limitation on the range from which they are drawn. [Limiting their range is also, of course, consistent with the context of declining school rolls.]

270 The process [of curriculum action] is not simple or easy, and it needs time. It is a process of evolution rather than instant change, in which the strengths of experience can be thoughtfully brought to bear on new needs as they are realised.

Summary

This is an impressive document which represents a substantial piece of research. It is difficult to fault its findings or its opinions, since they correspond with what informed observers have reported for some time. It also shows a firmer grasp of the idiom of secondary education, and a more sure-footed understanding of the key issues, than the HMI primary survey does of primary schools. Its conclusions cannot be seriously challenged and deserve to be influential. They may be reduced to two observations:

1 The curriculum of the English and Welsh secondary school – whether grammar, modern or comprehensive – is essentially that of the 1902 grammar school. The telltale features are:
    i a curriculum made up of separate subjects;
    ii the heavy use of option schemes as a way of making an essentially narrow curriculum more acceptable;

iii teaching methods which are didactic rather than interactive;
iv an emphasis on written work;
v neglect of performance subjects;
vi excessive importance attached to examinations;
vii grading of pupils to sort out the most academic, by means of setting and streaming devices often from the first year.

2 The variation in educational provision across the country, from one education authority to another, is extraordinarily great and affects both staffing levels and capitation.

The second conclusion is of major political significance but this has yet to be acted upon.[31] The survey does not draw the obvious conclusion: that the present system for administering education on a local basis leads to unacceptably low provision in many areas which cannot be rationally defended.[32] The first conclusion is confronted by the survey, which goes on to argue for curriculum planning so as to rethink the entire basis of secondary schooling. 'It is ultimately a more far-reaching matter of thinking through the implications of secondary education for all'. It recognises, too, that 'these questions bear directly upon the nature of the qualifications and the professionalism of teachers'. Their implications for in-service training are accepted.

In arguing for fewer options and a broader common curriculum, the secondary survey is on all fours with the Red Book and, for that matter, with the Green Paper doctrine of establishing a framework for the curriculum. But the survey is more realistic than either about the radical nature of the changes that are needed, and the complexity of curriculum action. The grosser simplicities of aims-objectives-implementation-assessment are not in evidence.

5 A Framework for the School Curriculum (1980)

This was the DES trial run for its national curriculum framework. It 'sets out preliminary views on the form the framework should take and the ground it should cover. . . . Comments will be welcomed from all concerned'. It has since been supplanted by its revised and final version, *The School Curriculum*. But it is worth a brief look, since it appears to have been little influenced by the generally more liberal views of HMI, and thus offers a glimpse of the thinking which finds favour with the DES civil servants.

It suggests a small core, made up of:

*E, M Not less than 10 per cent school time for each of these. Both are seen as 'organised policies . . . across the curriculum'.

S   A broad course until age 13, then 'integrated courses based on two or more of the specific science subjects may be appropriate'. At least 10, but not more than 20 per cent of the total time should be devoted to science subjects.

Re   LEAs are reminded of the compulsory provisions of the 1944 Act. But 'it is right, as is commonly the case, for Re to be linked with the wider consideration of personal and social values'. So Re need not be confined to a separate subject compartment.

Pe   Should 'normally be part of the curriculum': as with Re, no reason or explanation is offered, nor a time allocation.

(* See list of symbols in Appendix A.)

Despite this narrow, subject-based core, the document is elusive on the subject of options. Only modern languages are given a place in the sun: there should be a minimum of two, and preferably three years of teaching, amounting to about 10 per cent of school time. Some pupils should be able to learn more than one foreign language. 'Most pupils should have the opportunity to become acquainted with another modern European language as part of their secondary education'. But pupils should not normally devote more than 20 per cent of time to them, at any stage.

Most of the curriculum is banished to a brief section entitled 'Preparation for adult and working life'. Here, we read that 'many additions to the core subjects' are required: craft, design and technology; the arts (including Mu and D); H and G (separately, or 'as components in a programme of environmental and social education'); moral education, health education, preparation for parenthood; careers education, and 'preparation for a participatory role in adult society'. All these should 'at one stage or another . . . find a place in the education of every child', but 'the weight given to individual topics of this kind . . . should vary according to local circumstances and the ages and capabilities of the pupils'. So they are not part of the 11–16 core for all pupils.

Summary

Each pupil should follow 'a coherent and balanced programme', but the view of the core is not as broad nor as integrated as that of *Curriculum 11–16*. While modern languages are given enhanced status for no stated reason, important areas like aesthetic, expressive, social and moral education rest on an insecure basis. The document is reminiscent of the utilitarian, instrumental approach of Mr Callaghan's Ruskin speech and much of the subsequent Green Paper. It came in for much criticism from a variety of directions – particularly for its attempt to specify what proportion of time should be spent on some subjects. Its thinking is very much along subject lines and shows little trace of the broader reasoning which characterised *Curriculum 11–16*.

6   A View of the Curriculum (1980)

This HMI publication appeared within a few days of the DES *Framework*, and its timing suggests a bid by the Inspectorate to provide a counterpoise to the DES document. It offers suggestions which are 'positive rather than speculative', and appears to be a definitive statement of HMI opinion. It is, however, a disappointing document; its tired prose shows the scars of committee mutilation, and its only forthright opinions are disguised as 'Some propositions for consideration'. This presentation effectively deprives them of any real cutting edge. And where more detail is needed in order to make intentions clear – for instance, in the examples of curriculum structure – it is lacking.

Its importance, though, is due to the fact that it lies in the tradition instigated by *Curriculum 11–16*, and which ultimately was to influence *The School Curriculum*. The following extracts deal with its salient points:

Page
1   Teaching methods, the way schools manage their time and organise the use of buildings . . . and the way in which pupils are grouped . . . are not part of the curriculum. [An unfortunate beginning; means have been separated from ends – yet how you teach influences what you teach.]
6   The recent HMI surveys of primary and secondary education . . . indicate some unresolved problems. They essentially concern breadth, balance and coherence in the curriculum, and the relation of the parts to the whole. [This is now a familiar litany: but little further is said about how balance, breadth and coherence are to be conceptualised.]
11   Current practice is such that discussion on the primary school curriculum does not need to concern itself so much

with the total range of work as with the extent to which parts of the curriculum are developed, especially for able children. It is only provision of observational and experimental science that is seriously lacking in many primary schools . . . [In the wake of the HMI primary survey, this seems a curiously limited and complacent view. Coupled, as it is, with a further misleading section on 'skills' under the heading 'Content and concepts', it suggests a muddled view of the business and no clear idea of how to look at the curriculum as a whole.]

14–19 [The 'need to re-examine the rationale and organisational structure of the prevailing curriculum in many secondary schools' is dealt with by listing fourteen 'Propositions for Discussion'. These are paraphrased below, in a form which may be convenient for discussion groups.]

1 Explicit national consensus is needed on what constitutes 5 years of secondary education.
2 'Secondary education for all' implies a comparable range of learning for all: the common school implies a common curriculum.
3 Local variations in the school system ought not to affect the character and quality of the opportunities offered in schools. So policies and provision need to be consistent.
4 It is important to have a perspective for education from 14 to 18 as well as from 11 to 16.
5 There is need for more coherence within the experience of individual pupils. In current and traditional practice, curricula have commonly consisted of a number of discrete subjects: co-ordination of learning is hard to achieve. Policies which begin with a statement of assumptions about the learning to be achieved and which require the selection of components in light of those assumptions have a better prospect of attaining coherence in practice.
6 Since learning ultimately takes place through subjects, teachers must know what knowledge and skills subjects seek to promote. In integrated studies schemes learning outcomes must be clearly established.
7 A broader curriculum means a larger compulsory core in years 4 and 5, and fewer options made from fewer subjects.
8 All pupils need a broad kind of science education for all 5 years, to stimulate their minds and their imagination and equip them better for their future responsibilities as citizens.

Science, along with maths and CDT, helps develop understanding and appreciation of technology.

9 All pupils should learn a foreign language as part of the compulsory programme: it offers intellectual stimulus, cultural benefit and practical value.

10 All pupils' programmes should include aesthetic and creative experience. Social and political education should also be included, and may not be adequately covered by a choice of history, geography, economic or social or environmental studies.

11 A study of history should be maintained in the final secondary years. It is important to develop a historical perspective, and the necessary maturity is not usually attained by the age of 14.

12 The whole curriculum must be planned to offer all pupils personal and social development. Religious education; moral education; health education; community studies; careers education and an introduction to the environmental, economic and political concerns of the citizen all have a contribution to make, but not all need appear on the timetable as separate items.

13 Differentiation and choice are still needed. Subject areas in the compulsory core need not be treated identically for all pupils; there can be different levels of work, content and emphasis.

14 In the options, some new subjects can be offered, and compulsory studies extended or reinforced. Vocational subjects may be introduced.

Page

19–21 ['Two illustrations' are then offered of curriculums which meet 'some or all of the requirements sketched out above'. These are summarised below]:

Example A

Years 1 and 2   E, M, S, H, G, Re, Mu, A, Hk, CDT, Pe/Games and a foreign language for all pupils.

Year 3   All this, plus (i) careers, political and health ed., economic ed. and personal relationships; (ii) a second foreign language for some. Science is a balanced course. 'Some schools would choose to combine subjects formally in some interdisciplinary groupings.'

Years 4 and 5   *Core*: E, M, one science, one from H/G/So, one aesthetic/practical subject, Re, Pe, and careers/social education.

'Most pupils' continue with a foreign language. 'This core accounts for about two-thirds of the time.'
Options: these are taken from three groups. Two provide a second science, a second foreign language and other additional subjects. The third option offers short courses in computer studies, consumer education, childcare, work experience, private study, etc. as decided by school and pupil circumstances.

Summary
Years 1–3 are a broad-core programme for all pupils, but seen as contributing subjects rather than subsuming faculties. The second foreign language does not displace an existing subject, as in most present schemes; neither is there sex differentiation in art/craft. *Years 4–5* are virtually the Munn Report scheme, discussed below. The emphasis seems to be on subjects for their own sake. As in the DES *Framework*, the first foreign language is given quasi-core status. Three reasons are given for it: it offers 'intellectual stimulus', 'cultural benefit' and 'practical value, as our links with Europe and the rest of the world are strengthened'. Schools offering traditional core-plus-options curricula (as castigated in the HMI secondary survey) could move fairly painlessly to this scheme by establishing three 'core fields' of sciences, social studies and creative/aesthetic subjects; by pushing a foreign language as an option; by making two science subjects a maximum; and by enlarging the careers/health education element in their common core of E, M, Pe, Re and perhaps Se. Whether, however, such a scheme would in practice offer 'coherence within the experience of individual pupils' is by no means certain.

Example B
Years 1–3   As for Example A.
Years 4 and 5   A 'much broader' core: E, M, S, H, G, Re, A or Mu, Hk or CDT, Pe and Ca/Se. The aim is 'to embrace the essential elements of the subjects', and science 'is a balanced course for all'. 'The majority' continue with the first foreign language. About a quarter of the timetable is left for new subjects, or 'to extend or reinforce' compulsory subjects.

Summary
This is a high-level, big-core programme which achieves the same coverage as the Sheredes School scheme given in the case studies. It is difficult, indeed, to see how it can be done without subject integration and a faculty structure, and the emphasis here on

'breadth', 'essential elements' and 'balance' seems to confirm this. It is a pity, though, that these matters are not made more explicit. Both Examples A and B would satisfy the 'checklist' offered in *Curriculum 11–16*, but Example B has much more in common with the spirit of that document.

Looking back on this document, it is perhaps remarkable not for what it says, but for what it fails to say. In particular, it is extraordinary that two matters of critical importance in coherent planning of a common curriculum – the place of integration between subjects, and the grouping of pupils – are scarcely mentioned. There appears to be no reference to the link between ability grouping and pupil curriculums, in spite of the evidence of the HMI secondary survey that different sets and streams get a different curriculum. And the cursory mention of integration in Proposition 6 is largely obscured by a further reference to 'learning objectives'.

7   The School Curriculum (1981)

This is a short, well-written document which to some extent redeems the gaucheries of *Framework*. HMI influence is evident, and in many ways it is an improvement on *A View of the Curriculum*. It articulates a clearer view of curriculum activity, and endorses the argument for a common curriculum.[33]

But it has two major faults. First, it hardly fulfils the promise of Document 3, to offer a 'national consensus on a desirable framework for the curriculum'. There has been no deliberate and deliberative national discussion of the issues by any representative group; all that has happened is that a group of civil servants have invited comments on a first draft, listened to the HMI and produced some sleek prose. There has, for example, been no consultation with the Schools Council, which has been left to produce its own curriculum framework.

Second, the document therefore lacks the clarity and understanding which can only come from discussion with those who have direct knowledge of the issues and problems. And this is true of all seven documents: neither civil servants nor HMI have taken steps to involve in their discussions academics or teachers with core curriculum experience. So as soon as one probes beneath the surface of *The School Curriculum* to discover exactly what is meant and how it might be achieved, one finds blandness, confusion or evasion. Most critics of the document have disliked its platitudinous style: there is something to please everyone. But this is inevitable in a document written by people who quite simply do not know at first hand what they are talking about.

Circular 6/81, however, gives it great importance, and the extracts below draw attention to those sections which carry specific recommendations for whole curriculum planning:

Page
1   The school curriculum is at the heart of education . . .
      What is taught, and the way it is taught, should help all
      children to realise their potential to the fullest possible
      extent. [Not only is the curriculum of central importance. It
      is process as well as content: compare the more limited
      definition in *A View of the Curriculum*.]
4   New claims are always being made [for new subjects] . . .
      for the development of economic understanding,
      environmental education, preparation for parenthood,
      education for international understanding, political and
      social education, and consumer affairs. . . . But the time
      available to schools is limited. They have to devise
      priorities and to do so in a way which ensures that each
      pupil can be offered a broad programme, but one that
      includes what is essential and is coherent and balanced. . . .
      The schools can legitimately look to the further and higher
      sectors of education, and to parents and employers, to
      cover . . . those elements in the curriculum which they
      have not been able to include . . . and which others can
      provide as well or better. [Again, breadth, balance and
      coherence are the three virtues. And in pursuing them,
      schools must not bite off more than they can chew. This is
      an obscure passage which contradicts to an extent the
      principle (p.12) that 'School education needs to equip
      young people fully for adult and working life'. The lack of
      any clear rationale is evident again.] Examination
      syllabuses are not intended to be teaching syllabuses. . . .
      Examinations must be designed and used to serve the
      educational process. [Useful ammunition against those who
      put the exam cart before the curriculum horse.]
6   Three . . . issues deserve special mention. . . . First . . .
      there is now among pupils and parents a greater diversity of
      personal values. Second, the effect of technology on
      employment patterns sets a new premium on adaptability,
      self-reliance and other personal qualities. Third . . . it is

essential to ensure that equal curricular opportunity is genuinely available to both boys and girls. [Multi-cultural aspects; person-centred view of education; equal treatment of sexes.]

7   Breadth . . . is commonly defined in terms of subjects [which can] . . . help to broaden every pupil's education if they are provided in appropriate depth and combinations. [There follows a list of several subjects and their contributions: H, G, Ec, Gk, L, A, Mu, Dr, Pe, Hk, CDT. The inclusion of Gk and L as 'classical languages', though, suggests that these are not all seen as core subjects.] Essential constituents . . . concern personal and social development . . . under the headings of moral education, health education [including sex education] and preparation for parenthood and family life. [PSD is thus identified as a core curriculum component, but these areas 'may be more effectively covered if they are distributed across the curriculum'. This argues against Design for Living and similar courses.]

8   Religious education . . . has a distinctive contribution to make . . . and can help pupils to understand the religious and cultural diversity of contemporary society. [An interesting contrast with the position in the USA, where cultural diversity *excludes* Re from the curriculum.] Throughout primary and secondary education . . . the curriculum needs to be viewed as a whole. . . . Each pupil's programme should be balanced and meet his personal needs as he progresses. [A welcome emphasis on whole curriculum planning; but 'pupils' needs' is a tricky concept, and an unsatisfactory basis for a curriculum.[34] Its use here is maladroit.]

10 Primary schools . . . must provide a wide range of experience. . . . There is no evidence that a narrow curriculum, concentrating only on the basic skills, enables children to do better in these skills. [Another welcome emphasis.]

11 *Topic work*: primary schools . . . should have a clear overall plan for work of this kind . . .
    Science: primary schools should provide more effective science teaching. . . . More [effort] is needed . . .

12 *Art and craft*: primary schools . . . [should encourage] direct observation and study [and] the development of skills and inventiveness in producing artefacts . . .

French: primary schools should seek to introduce or
maintain the teaching of a modern language only where
continuing teaching expertise and co-ordination with
secondary schools are assured.
[These four specific points stem from the HMI primary
survey, but with even more emphasis on primary science. Is
it not possible, though, that primary science may in due
course lead to exactly the same strictures as are now made
for primary French?]

12 The Secretaries of State wish to emphasise three
propositions about secondary education . . .

  i Schools should plan their curriculum as a whole . . . [it]
  should not be simply a collection of separate
  subjects . . .

  ii There is an overwhelming case for providing all pupils
  between 11 and 16 with curricula of a broadly common
  character . . .

  iii Young people . . . must be able to see where their
  education has meaning outside school.

[These are the frame factors for the comprehensive
curriculum.]

13 The choice [at age 14] must be so managed that pupils'
secondary schooling does not suffer. Pupils should not drop
potentially valuable subjects before they are mature
enough to understand their importance . . . [The days of
free-for-all option systems are numbered.]

  Although choices . . . have to be made at the end of the
third year, every pupil up to 16 should sustain a broad
curriculum. The level, content and emphasis of work will be
related to pupils' abilities and aspirations, but there should
be substantial common elements. [The list is as follows: E,
M, S, Re, Pe; 'some study of the humanities';
'opportunities for some practical and some aesthetic
activity'; 'Most pupils should study a foreign language, and
many should . . . through the whole five-year period.'
The special status given to languages in *Framework* is
eased. In the humanities and techno-aesthetic areas, 'some
study' and 'opportunities' are vague enough to cover a
range of patterns, from geography and woodwork, through
to an integrated humanities course and an integrated design
course. Taken with the earlier mention of PSD, this list
matches the approach of *A View of the Curriculum* in both
breadth and ambiguity.]

14   Every school should ensure that each pupil's programme
includes a substantial and well-distributed time allocation
for English, mathematics and science up to age 16. . . . It is
for the local education authorities . . . to suggest minimum
time allocations in these subjects . . . [The secondary
survey revealed that bipartite structures for the curriculum
were depriving less able pupils of maths and science in years
4 and 5. The minimum allocations in *Framework* have been
dropped, but so also have the upper limits. This is perhaps a
pity, since some schools may be encouraged to require
some pupils to take three science subjects, or two
languages, or both. The failure to explain 'balance' is no
help here.]

English . . . is a necessary concern of all teachers and there
needs to be an organised policy for English across the
curriculum. [This is conventional Bullock rhetoric: the
secondary survey pointed to the difficulty of giving
'language across the curriculum' much meaning. The stress
on English as a separate subject is unfortunate, since it may
discourage schools from making it a part – with its own
identity – of 11–16 humanities schemes.]

Mathematics . . . is the key to much human knowledge and
understanding . . . [This seems a bold claim:[35] it is a pity as
much prominence is not given to the humanities as such.]

15   *Science* . . . [is] an essential component of education for all
pupils of 11 to 16 . . .

  a Syllabuses must . . . take further the ideas which need
to be introduced at the primary stage . . .

  b Courses for pupils up to 16 need . . . to ensure a
reasonable balance across the sciences. . . . Many
examination syllabuses . . . are overloaded . . .

  c [To avoid premature dropping of science subjects,
pupils should] continue with some work in the three
main sciences in the fourth and fifth years, and there
are those who argue that for all pupils, including the
less able, a scientific education requires a programme
of this breadth.

  d Science teachers [are not well equipped] . . . for
teaching outside their own specialism . . .

  e Science . . . can be accommodated in the 11–16
curriculum on the required scale . . . only if courses
can be developed which [do not make] . . .
unacceptable demands on curriculum time.

[This section is a clear pointer towards unified science programmes at both single and double subject level. It should be of some help to schools planning such courses, and needing support in meeting the objections of some parents and employers.]

Modern languages provision as a whole [should be] planned by the local education authority across its area. . . . Similar consideration [may be needed for] classical languages. [A number of further points are made: what is the value of present modern language courses; should they be linguistic or cultural; how important is course length and class ability range? For languages, as for science, the document declares that the DES will take these issues further and publish conclusions in due course. The need to rationalise modern languages provision is long overdue; but many LEAs have no adviser for them, let alone for classical languages. How well is this likely to be done?]

Microelectronics . . . [are likely to transform] many aspects of adult life and work. . . . Pupils should become familiar with the use and application of computers, particularly through direct experience . . . [This seems to be urging 'hands-on' experience, along with knowledge of applications. The social effects of these devices do not seem to be regarded as equally important for curriculum discussion.]

Craft, design and technology [is] . . . part of the preparation for living and working in modern industrial society . . . [it] encourages creative skills [and can] enrich and add interest to what is taught in other subjects . . . [CDT is given 'special importance' by the Secretaries of State. The claims made for it here can be met only if it is taught imaginatively; again, more clarity about what CDT might mean in the curriculum would be helpful. It can easily become heavily materials-focused and teacher-directed, and little more than a kind of applied science, aimed all too consciously at 'the world of work' and offering little real intellectual development.]

Preparation for adult life . . . is a major function of the schools, [to be] reflected in the whole of their curriculum. [This section has a heavy instrumental emphasis: there is much about relating the curriculum 'to what happens outside schools', to 'the wealth-creating process', to 'better careers education', to 'links with industry'. This dates from the Ruskin speech, and if taken at face value could distort the curriculum severely. It is also difficult to reconcile with the earlier emphasis on the need for adaptability in a changing world; the emphasis seems to be on preparing pupils for the world as it is, rather than giving them the kind of personal autonomy that will equip them for the world only they will know.]

20 Schools should . . . analyse and set out their aims in writing, and make it part of their work regularly to assess how far the education they provide matches those aims. [This harks back to the objectives model of the curriculum which runs through *Curriculum 11–16*, and clearly finds favour with the DES bureaucrats.]

In retrospect, the seven documents are more notable for what they have in common than for their differences. Although the professional background of HMI leads to some occasional differences of emphasis, *The School Curriculum* gives the game away. The same political end is in view: a top-down core curriculum programme, using a managerial, objectives-based model of control and with no additional resources. Moreover, the same 1960s-style growth model of the economy is assumed, from the Green Paper onwards: there is no hint that new technology might necessitate new industrial scenarios. The curriculum is to serve society as it is.[36]

Nevertheless, for whatever wrong reasons and with whatever false accents, *Aspects of Secondary Education* shows beyond doubt that the case for a big-core, high-level common curriculum is unassailable: it is simply the case for a proper comprehensive curriculum. The best strategy, therefore, is to make the most of an indifferent job; to make use of those parts of *The School Curriculum* which are unexceptionable, re-interpret those which are not, and produce defensible arguments for any serious deviations. Rather than carp at the patent infelicities of the DES document, we can recognise its strengths and look closely at exactly what is being said. Then we can get on with the task of developing a rationale in each school and solving the problems which arise.

Two associated documents

The next chapter will look more closely at these tasks. I shall conclude this chapter with a look at two more government documents on curriculum, but which lie outside the sequence I have examined above. The first of these appeared in Scotland at the same time as the 1977 DES Green Paper for England and Wales. These matters are ordered differently in Scotland, and this report is the work not of HMI or civil servants, but of a committee made up of heads, teachers, lecturers, advisers and examination board officials as well as HMI, and chaired by the headteacher of a secondary school. It is generally known as the Munn Report after its chairman, but its full title is *The Structure of the Curriculum in the Third and Fourth Years of the Scottish Secondary School*. Its focus is the Scottish equivalent of years 4 and 5 in the English secondary school, but the breadth of its analysis makes it equivalent to *The School Curriculum*, five years earlier and in many ways better.[37]

1   The Munn Report (1977)

There is not space to analyse the report in detail. But it recognises at the beginning that 'the concept of balance is itself an elusive one', and that claims to influence curriculum design are made from considerations of society, of knowledge and of how pupils learn. In the light of these, four sets of aims are arrived at (see next chapter); from these, eight 'modes of activity' are established:

Munn: modes of activity	*Red Book: areas of experience*
Linguistic and literary study	The linguistic
Mathematical studies	The mathematical
Scientific study	The scientific
Social studies	The social and political
Creative and aesthetic activities	The aesthetic and creative
	The physical
Physical activity	The spiritual
Religious studies	The ethical
Morality	

Comparison of the Munn modes with the Red Book's areas shows total identity; yet neither refers to the other, nor to any other source for this exercise in epistemology. The great merit of Munn, however, is that at least a rationale is offered to account for the eight modes; so it must be assumed that the Munn committee originated this Hirstian treatment of curriculum structure, and that the English HMIs made unacknowledged use of it. The point is that any school planning a curriculum design by means of the Red Book's eight areas ought to take account of chapters 1 to 4 of the Munn Report: and ideally, of Hirst's 1965 paper too.

The Munn Report goes on to confront with admirable forthrightness the next question: should there be 'a subject-based approach on the one hand' or 'an "integrated" or inter-disciplinary approach on the other?' In the event, it concludes that 'the basic unit of study should remain the individual subject; but this recommendation needs to be qualified in a number of ways'. These may be summarised:

1   To reduce 'excessive fragmentation in the curriculum', larger blocks of time than 35–40 minute periods are desirable;
2   Subjects should not be taught in a narrow way, but 'as resources for the development of conceptual understanding, social competence, and a wide range of skills and emotional and moral attitudes'. This makes a sharp comparison with the DES tendency to hive off a separate area of 'personal and social development', and yet not make clear how it is to be 'distributed across the curriculum' (*The School Curriculum*). The Munn approach is clear and direct. Furthermore, Munn recognises the dangers of a subject-based approach in a key passage: 'The contributions of the different subjects [should be] so orchestrated that, in their different ways, they lead to the . . . aims of the school. This . . . will be vitiated from the start, and the curriculum reduced to a haphazard collection of disjointed units, if subject departments, insisting on their own autonomy, simply go their separate ways.'
3   Subjects should not be 'wholly self-contained'. Attention should be paid to 'the relationships between the various subjects. . . . A more systematic attempt at co-ordination is required . . . if proper attention is to be given to multi-disciplinary issues'.

Finally, before outlining a model of the curriculum, Munn tackles the matter of pupil grouping. It advises that 'the social, educational, and prognostic value' of mixed ability classes in the first year (corresponding to the English second year) 'can be very great', and further that 'The arguments which can be adduced against streaming upon entry to the secondary school' amount to 'a strong case for the prolongation of the "orientation and assessment" period into S2' (our third year). Some setting is seen as 'perfectly acceptable', but none the less this passage represents a powerful endorsement of the view that mixed ability work should be the major feature of 11–14 education. This impressive recommendation makes a strong contrast with the DES treatment of the matter which is to ignore it.

TABLE 1.1

	CORE AREA			ELECTIVE AREA
Fixed core	*One subject from each of 3 core fields*			
Take all subjects *14	Social Studies 4	Science 4	Creative Arts 4	Choose 2 or 3 subjects 14
E M	Ec, H, G, 'Modern Studies' (All to include a module or modules based on a study of contemporary society)	B, C, P, General Science, Engineering Science, Food Science	A, Mu, Dr, Dance, Creative Craft	F, Gm, Sp, Ln, B, C, P, G, H, Td, Mk, Wk, Hk, Nk, A, Pe, Re, Modern Studies, Accounting, Secretarial Studies, etc.

* Minimum period allocations in a 40-period week.

Notes

1 'Food Science' and 'Creative Craft' are examples of collaborative courses between Hk, technical, and S or A;
2 In Creative Arts, short courses 'will enable pupils . . . to gain experience of more than one of the activities';
3 6 periods remain unallocated as a 'flexibility element'.

It will readily be seen that Example A of *A View of the Curriculum* is a Munn look-alike. If such a scheme were to be implemented with due regard to the Munn qualifications about the dangers of trying to assemble a common curriculum from isolated subject elements, it might offer balance and coherence. In practice, it is hard to see what will stop subject departments going 'their separate ways' without some form of faculty structure, since the curriculum design, in the end, has not been translated into a firm structure but is rather left as a set of policies. In any event, it is not easy to see how choosing just one science subject – whichever it is – will give pupils an understanding of science as an aspect of our culture. And the same argument applies to each of the other two core fields.

The Munn Report is therefore a flawed document, but its analysis of whole curriculum planning makes it important to anyone seriously embarking on this kind of design. And because Munn-type schemes can easily be constructed – in substance, if not in spirit – from existing core-plus-option schemes, they are likely to become numerous. It is worth adding, though, that the Munn proposals have been rejected by the largest Scottish teachers' organisation because it is 'an extremely conservative document' which 'does not go far enough'.[38]

2 Curriculum 11–16: A Review of Progress (1981)

The second document worth examination was published by the DES in 1981 by HMSO, and is described as 'A joint study by HMI and five LEAs'. It is a sequel to the Red Book, and describes 'an enquiry' carried out by 41 schools in 5 LEAs with a group of HMI over the three years following the Red Book's publication; and it is seen as 'relevant to actions that need to follow the Government's paper' (*The School Curriculum*). It is therefore relevant to us here.

It has to be said that the book makes heavy reading, and that the results of the 'enquiry' do not seem to amount to very much. An enormous amount of talk and paper appear to have brought forth a mouse. It is nowhere clear that all this effort has led to any significant curriculum change in any of the schools concerned. We read that 'work in the schools has not yet reached a stage where changes in classroom practice or policy can be identified clearly or assessed systematically. Valuable conclusions may nevertheless be drawn about fruitful and unfruitful lines of inquiry. . . . ' In view of the high-powered nature of this sustained exercise, we need to know why it has achieved so little.

For instance, in the critical area of years 4 and 5, it emerges that 'the most frequent way in which schools tried to achieve a more balanced programme for all pupils was to group subjects together within an area such as 'sciences', 'humanities' or 'aesthetic/ creative', and to stipulate that pupils should study at least one subject from each of these areas'. Thus all the inquiry seems to have achieved is merely the adoption of a straightforward Munn model, with all the inherent disadvantages discussed above.

It seems likely that the main reason for this failure lies in the implicit managerialism and explicit objectives model of the curriculum presented in the Red Book itself – and reproduced in all the subsequent publications. For the representative of one of the five LEAs is quoted as seeing the inquiry as 'the description and evaluation of the curriculum using the Red Book as a framework for looking at actual practice'. Others noted that there was a danger in 'too facile a treatment of the checklist', and that time 'had been spent in routine organisation and administration, instead of thinking about the curriculum'. The most revealing insight into the inquiry comes from the report on its future plans: 'Schools . . . would evaluate aspects of their provision, from overall curricular policy to departmental aims and objectives. . . . This evaluation would involve the construction, analysis and testing of curriculum patterns.' The language of scientific management is still more evident in the recommended programme for schools to begin their own curriculum inquiry:

a   Schools would examine their existing curriculum . . . [to] provide a basis of factual information;
b   Schools would identify aims and objectives . . .
c   Schools would then be led on to . . . pedagogic principles and classroom techniques . . . assessment of pupils; evaluation, both internal and external.

The process of change is viewed in the same linear, procedural way. One head's 'analysis' is given prominence:

To clarify the purposes of change.
To define the means . . .
To decide criteria for assessing . . .
To match them with the school's stated objectives.
To support and prepare staff . . .
To develop a school management system . . .
To encourage a problem-solving approach . . .
To arrange for effective links between the curriculum group and the school management system . . .
To arrange for regular progress reports . . .
To arrange for planned, regular evaluation of the process of change, using the previously agreed criteria.

This approach to the tasks of curriculum planning runs through the entire exercise. The failure of the exercise to come up with anything very much may have something to do with this needlessly exclusive view of how to manage change. It would be a pity to saddle schools with it just at the time when industry is rejecting it in favour of more devolved styles of management. The next chapter will take this point further. But it should be noted that words like 'objectives', 'system', and 'planned evaluation' usually indicate that thinking and judgment are under threat from empty procedures.

The report is, however, not without some useful information. There is a helpful tabulation (p.44) of time allocations to different subjects in the schools studied which plugs one of the few gaps – and a surprising one – in the HMI secondary survey. For instance, the percentage of the week timetabled for first year science can vary from 7.5 to 12. In curriculum planning it is important to know one's degree of freedom; the traditional base of accepted practice from which one must start. Table 1.2 is reproduced from the document.

TABLE 1.2 *Time allocations in the first year*

Subject	Average	Highest	Lowest
English	*14	15[1]	10
Mathematics	13.7	15[2]	10
Science	12	17	7.5
Humanities[3]	13	17.5	10
Creative/aesthetic[4]	18.7	30	12
Modern language	12	15	8.5
Physical education[5]	9.7	12.5	5

* Times are given as a percentage of the timetabled week.

Notes
1 The amount of English recorded for slow learning pupils in two schools exceeded this, the highest being 20 per cent.
2 The amount of mathematics recorded for slow learning pupils in two schools exceeded this, the highest being 20 per cent.
3 Humanities includes combined humanities courses, separate history and geography and courses such as Man: A Course of Study (MACOS) (1 school) and Inter-Disciplinary Enquiry (IDE) (2 schools).
4 Creative/aesthetic studies include time allocated to Craft, Design and Technology (CDT), home economics, needlework, art, music and drama.
5 Including games.
(Taken from *Curriculum 11–16: A Review of Progress*, HMSO, 1981.)

Some of the variations listed in this table are quite striking, and the reader will notice similar variations – not only in the first year, but in all 11–16 years – in the allocations of the seven schools examined in the case studies of Chapter 3.

The document is of further value, since some interesting comments on the actual process of change may be found embedded in the commentary:

Page
57 Many teachers had found it hard to come to grips with the idea that they could be the agents for developing the curriculum. . . . [There was] the feeling of many teachers that in undertaking any kind of curriculum reappraisal they were at the limit of their experience and capacity.

60 The attempt to review a subject's possible contribution to the curriculum could lead to artificial exercises in justification 'with subjects dredging deep to find some form of response under all eight headings'.

62 The style of the head's leadership could be a vital factor in encouraging teachers to identify with the work.

63 Much communication within the exercise had been on paper. This had posed problems for many teachers, who felt that there had been too much to read . . .

What also emerges from the report is the value to schools of external support agents, even though 'the availability of HMI had been rather uneven'. It is difficult to avoid the conclusion that the combination of LEA advisers and HMI probably increased the amount of paper in circulation. Each belong to organisations which require that informal contact be supported by documentation. It is interesting, too, that 'Initially, teachers had felt some doubts about the idea of working with HMI and advisers – who in their minds, were not always distinguished from each other.' This tends to confirm research into the conflict inherent in the adviser's role: the conflict between the adviser and the inspector. The passage suggests that schools eye the adviser with the same wariness as Her Majesty's Inspector, and this has important implications for the capacity of advisers to act as effective support agents for curriculum change.[39] Yet Circular 6/81 places on LEAs the responsibility of 'securing a planned and coherent curriculum within the schools' – that is, of large-scale whole curriculum change as advocated in *The School Curriculum*. It is likely that not only much more school-based in-service help will be needed, but also fresh thinking about the kind of support agencies that can assist the process of regenerating the curriculum.

Exercise 1: rethinking the school curriculum

The outline programme presented here is an attempt to suggest how a school – or group of schools – might rethink its curriculum in the light of the considerations discussed above. The aim is to avoid the approach criticised in this chapter, which seeks to define the curriculum as objectives derived from aims, and then to evaluate practice against these objectives. Instead, it is argued that we need to promote reflection on practice, and to view the curriculum as a whole.

It is tempting to suppose that the task of designing a curriculum is no different in kind from that of designing a heat exchanger, and those who take a deterministic view of things will search for the equivalent in curriculum theory of theories of heat transfer. The argument of Chapter 1 is that these scientistic analogies are invalid: we are dealing with a class of problems which yields to general methods rather than inviolate principles. The approach set out as the exercise below postulates a series of steps which form a tentative method of linking design and implementation in an organised fashion:

1   a statement of aim or purpose is needed: not as the basis for detailed objectives, but as a way of establishing shared beliefs and values, and thus forming a rationale for the curriculum – for example, that pupils should acquire personal autonomy;
2   we need a way of identifying knowledge fields – hence the value of attempts to descry disciplines, areas, forms and fields of knowledge. But we must be clearer on what basis they rest;
3   in recognising the cultural ambiguities within liberal education, we need a method – that of deliberation is advocated here;
4   we need a school structure, flexible enough to respond to a variety of learning strategies and to changing interpretations of subjects as cultural elements – hence the case (examined in the next section) – for faculties and a mixed-ability format;
5   we need school-based curriculum development, coupled with an extended notion of teacher professionalism so that subjects can be used not as ends in themselves but as means to further ends;
6   we can then apply these methods to the curriculum problems which we recognise within a given kind of school activity;
7   in this way, curriculum decisions are properly contextualised

and the relevant data are brought to bear on the process of decision-making.

A school might work through the following programme because it is being reorganised, or reduced in size, or simply because its staff have decided to look again at the curriculum it offers.

It is suggested that each of the four phases might take about a term to complete.

Phase 1: orientation

The aim is to develop a fresh point of view by looking outside the school. It is carried out chiefly by embarking on a programme of visits to other schools. Most of the schools will be within twenty miles or so, and will have been chosen because of some particular feature: use of learning resources, mixed ability work, integrated studies, remedial organisation, etc. Perhaps one or two trips will be arranged to schools in another LEA but with an outstanding curriculum development under way.

While some simple form of checklist might help prepare staff for the visits, too much detail should be avoided, and care should be taken not to give the host school the impression that some kind of evaluation is under way. It is helpful to let the host school know in advance what the focus of the visit will be. It is essential that, after the visit, some form of report is prepared on what has been seen and noted. There are advantages in both oral and written accounts. Oral reports might be given at a brief after-school meeting, or even in morning break in the staffroom if time presses. Written reports can be a collective summary by the visiting group, or individual accounts. Length is less important than a prompt, informed response which can be distributed to staff and used in later phases of deliberation.

As a complement to the programme of visits – or, if necessary, a substitute for some of them – a simulation study like that presented at the end of Chapter 2 here may be a useful stimulus. The questions underpinning each school visit are:

What is this school trying to do?
In what ways is it succeeding?
In what ways is it less satisfactory?
What ideals does it offer?
Which of its approaches are of interest?

Phase 2: concepts and strategies

The emphasis here is on the task of curriculum building. The aim is to see the curriculum as a whole, and recognise the unity of design and implementation.

A programme of after-school sessions would be advantageous, combining general inputs with a working party structure. The intention is to give staff an opportunity to pursue their particular concerns, but at the same time retain the whole curriculum as a focus. Three strands could make up this phase:

1   *Lectures*: from two to four lectures, dealing with general topics of curriculum and organisation, could be arranged for all staff. These would draw on a variety of sources: heads of neighbouring schools; lecturers from a nearby higher education institution; members of the school's own staff with an interesting view to put forward.

2   *Working parties*: staff will be free to join working parties tackling specific issues. There is a difficulty here: too many themes will mean a fragmented approach, and this will make it harder to draw the threads together. The list of working parties given below deliberately deals with four overlapping themes, so that there is common ground between them, and therefore a common basis for subsequent discussion. The working parties should not be restricted to teachers representing particular levels of responsibility, or particular specialisms, or particular schools where more than one school is involved. The aim is to form general principles and concepts which might act as a guide to decision-making, not to frame formal solutions reflecting specific constraints.

3   *Case study structures*: a valuable way of retaining the focus on the whole curriculum is to use case studies of actual schools as support material during this phase. These could be obtained as a result of the visits in Phase 1, or by using published material such as that presented in Chapter 3 of this book. In this way staff can locate their individual concerns in a wider context by using the case studies as the basis for critical discussion.

Phase 3: formation

The ideal setting for launching this phase of the operation is a residential conference. If the LEA is unable to provide this kind of help, it is possible (although less satisfactory) to use the school itself as the base for a non-residential weekend conference. There are many different ways in which this part of the programme might be arranged, depending on the nature of the task and the opportunities available. An opening conference of leading staff might set out a draft curriculum structure, in the light of the recommendations produced by the working parties in Phase 2. A subsequent day conference of all staff might consider these proposals, identify points of support and dissent, and then these might be resolved in a final conference after formal and informal discussion. A series of after-school sessions will be needed to study the implications of the proposals, determine problems and frame alternative solutions, and specify necessary resources and broad intentions. At this stage, the sessions might most profitably be arranged as working parties which bring together, for the first time, staff with common interests: specific departments or faculties, specific responsibilities.

Phase 4: consolidation

The task is now to devise strategies by which the agreed programme may be implemented. Teaching materials will need to be produced or purchased, or adapted; staff teams will be formed; funding will be procured for priority needs; timetable structures will be developed and agreed. The emphasis will be on informal, workshop settings; staff will undertake a substantial amount of work, knowing that it has been possible to put forward all views and place them in the setting of the curriculum as a whole and the shared intentions and values which it seeks to present.

Working parties for Phase 2

It is suggested that, in larger schools, parallel working parties should be established under the same heading. There is much to be said for more than one group producing solutions to the same problems. Much can be gained from discussing alternative proposals; it is an ideal setting for staff to discover each other's ideas and predilections, and to expose assumptions to critical debate.

Problems and prescriptions: the curriculum context

Working party A: curriculum structure

Briefing tasks:

1 What rationale should underpin the curriculum?
2 In what way (subjects, faculties, curriculum areas) should the 11–16 curriculum be formulated?
3 How should the school day and period length be arranged?
4 How should specific problems (options, foreign languages, science) be tackled?
5 How should curriculum relate to pastoral structures?
6 What are the implications for curriculum process?

Working party B: subjects and the curriculum

Briefing tasks:

1 What rationale should underpin the curriculum?
2 How might subjects be used so as to promote curriculum coherence?
3 What forms of interrelation between subjects might be appropriate?
4 What are the implications for timetabling and the school day?
5 What are the implications for pupil grouping?
6 What are the implications for resources?

Working party C: the learning process

Briefing tasks:

1 How can existing subjects form the basis for the whole curriculum?
2 What form of pupil grouping is advisable?
3 What resources for learning are needed?
4 What reprographic provision is indicated?
5 What are the implications for pupil records and assessment?
6 What are the implications for pastoral structures?
7 What learning strategies are appropriate to the needs of the entire ability range?

Working party D: Pupils, parents and society

Briefing tasks:

1 How might curriculum and organisation best promote personal, social and moral development?
2 How should the pastoral care structure relate to pupil records, sanctions, counselling, assemblies and reports?
3 How should the curriculum take account of careers guidance and the world of work in general?
4 What forms of accountability are likely to be acceptable and helpful to parents?

In this exercise, the reader is invited to consider whether the approach outlined above is a helpful one, and to reflect upon the specific responses which might be made to the questions listed above as tasks for the working parties.

Chapter 2

Strategies and structures: approaches to curriculum change

It is one thing to list the desirable attributes and ingredients of a curriculum; quite another to implement it when the prevailing curriculum is markedly at odds with what is being recommended. In this part of the book, I shall look at ways in which change might, or might not, be fostered, and draw attention to some specific issues which arise from the documents summarised in Chapter 1.

At the end of this chapter a simulation exercise is offered, based on a fictitious school. The existing curriculum is displayed, using a form of curriculum notation which is becoming common and which is explained in Appendix B. The reader is invited to assume the place of an incoming head, keen to reshape the curriculum – not least because of the pressure of falling rolls. The result might then be compared with some of the actual examples of curriculum structures presented in Chapter 3.

For the moment, it is convenient to look at this exercise and the present curriculum at Brobdingnag School in order to see what assumptions are present and what might be the scale of change. For although this mythical school corresponds to no school I know of, it incorporates features which may be seen in most existing secondary schools.[1] It is an attempt to exemplify the kind of curriculum which comes in for robust criticism in the HMI secondary survey. Its key features are: (see p.103)

1 the curriculum is seen as a collection of subjects. Even careers, social and health education are reduced to the 'subject' of 'design for living' in years 4 and 5. Where options exist, pupils choose without reference to any rationale of what they ought to be learning about;

2 different curricula are offered to different pupils. Those in the

upper band have more subjects and more choice. But is either group of pupils being offered a good curriculum?

3   even within the bands, pupils are heavily differentiated by supposed ability. Those of whom the system has low expectations are likely to respond accordingly;

4   pupils view each subject in isolation, and it is seen as an end in itself rather than a means to some further educational end. Under these conditions it is easy for subject examinations to become more important than the process of subject teaching.

All these features make some sort of sense only if the purpose of schooling is to identify and train a small elite to carry out academic operations in some specialised subject: that is, to acquire that very narrow kind of excellence which secures open awards at ancient universities. It was always a formula for a restricted curriculum, and the grammar schools were not particularly good at working it (as the Crowther Report of 1959 revealed).[2] But it is plainly a very unsatisfactory basis for a curriculum intended to educate all our pupils for a demanding and unpredictable world.

Aims: how elaborate should they be?

One obvious way of devising a new curriculum is to set out detailed aims in writing. Chapter 1 shows how this approach runs through the HMI and DES documents from 1977 to date. It sounds logical and tidy to write down aims and go from these to more specific objectives. Exercise 2 looks at the business more closely.

Exercise 2: aims in education

A   The following 'aims of the schools' are listed in the 1977 Green Paper:

  i   to help children develop lively, inquiring minds; giving them the ability to question and to argue rationally, and to apply themselves to tasks;

  ii   to instil respect for moral values, for other people and for oneself, and tolerance of other races, religions, and ways of life;

  iii   to help children understand the world in which we live, and the interdependence of nations;

61

iv to help children to use language effectively and imaginatively in reading, writing and speaking;

v to help children appreciate how the nation earns and maintains its standard of living and properly to esteem the essential role of industry and commerce in this process;

vi to provide a basis of mathematical, scientific and technical knowledge, enabling boys and girls to learn the essential skills needed in a fast changing world of work;

vii to teach children about human achievement and aspirations in the arts and sciences, in religion, and in the search for a more just social order;

viii to encourage and foster the development of the children whose social or environmental disadvantages cripple their capacity to learn, if necessary by making additional resources available to them.

B The above statement was produced under a Labour administration. In 1980, the DES document *Framework for the School Curriculum*, under a Conservative administration, listed the following aims, which were commended, without alteration, in *The School Curriculum* (1981):

i to help pupils develop lively, inquiring minds, the ability to question and argue rationally and to apply themselves to tasks, and physical skills;

ii to help pupils acquire knowledge and skills relevant to adult life and employment in a fast-changing world;

iii to help pupils use language and number effectively;

iv to instil respect for religious and moral values, and tolerance of other races, religions, and ways of life;

v to help pupils understand the world in which they live, and the interdependence of individuals, groups and nations;

vi to help pupils appreciate human achievements and aspirations.

The same document also states: 'Schools are likely to be more effective in achieving their curricular aims if these aims are clearly set out in writing . . . and interpreted in more specific objectives . . . '.

C The Scottish Munn Report (1977) identifies four sets of aims:

i The first set of aims involves the development of knowledge and understanding, both of the self and of the social and physical environment . . . To explore the ways in which pupils themselves relate to others . . . to help pupils understand the way of life of their own society . . .

ii The second set of aims is concerned with skills . . . The ability to read, to handle numbers . . . to hypothesise, to enquire . . . to criticise and to create . . . to get on with others . . . to carry out experiments, to cook, to make objects, to express oneself through music . . .

iii The third set is concerned with . . . emotional and moral development . . . to be concerned for other people and to show compassion for them . . . to respect evidence . . . to be resourceful, self-reliant and hard-working . . . to have an open attitude to social change . . . to go on improving their capacities . . .

iv The fourth set of aims is concerned with the demands of society . . . Schools have an inescapable duty to ensure that young people are equipped to perform the various roles which life in their society entails . . .

D The document *Core Curriculum for Australian Schools* (1980) lists four 'universal aims of education':

i the nurturing and development of the powers of reasoning, reflective and critical thinking, imagining, feeling and communicating among and between persons;

ii the maintenance, development and renewal (and not merely the preservation) of the culture; that is of our forms and systems of thought, meaning and expression – such as scientific knowledge, the arts, language and technology;

iii the maintenance, development and renewal (and not merely the preservation) of the social, economic and political order – including its underlying values, fundamental structures and institutions;

iv the promotion of mental, physical, spiritual and emotional health in all people.

1 Compare the Green Paper aims with those listed in *The School Curriculum*. Are there signs of common parentage?

2 Aim A(v) has been dropped from the B version. Is it educational or political in nature? Why should a Labour education secretary endorse industry's influence, and a Conservative secretary play it down? What might the word 'esteem' mean?

3   Aim A(viii) has also been dropped. Should aims seek to specify in particular detail?
4   How might a teacher 'instil respect' for religious and moral values? Can one 'instil . . . tolerance of other races'? What educational meaning can we give to the activity of instilling?
5   Compare B and C. Are these aims statements broadly of the same character? Are there items which arise in one and not the other?
6   Consider D. Do these aims differ again from both B and C? Do they disclose any preoccupations not evident in B or C?
7   Which of the four aims statements is of most educational merit?

The function of aims

It is perhaps clear that there are as many different ways of preparing statements of aims as there are of skinning a cat. What is more, aims can be as much political as educational in intent. If one must have written aims, there may be much to be said for making them as brief as possible. Those given in the Warnock Report (1978) are succinct, and were endorsed as curriculum aims by the HMI document *A View of the Curriculum*:

> First, to enlarge a child's knowledge, experience and imaginative understanding, and thus his awareness of moral values and capacity for enjoyment; and secondly, to enable him to enter the world after formal education is over as an active participant in society and a responsible contributor to it, capable of achieving as much independence as possible.

This statement preserves the classic duality: the first aim is to do with the self, the second with self and society. But might not the single aim of developing personal autonomy suffice?[3] Warnock emphasises 'as much independence as possible'; to be autonomous is not to be ungovernable, but to wish to be governed in certain ways. There is evidently room for endless philosophical dispute on such matters.

One might go further, and question whether the need to write down a statement of aims is not itself an admission of failure. Doctors, after all, recognise that their duty is to cure the sick; they do not require a written statement of aims before they begin work.[4] Should not the aim of a teacher to educate be taken as an implicit part of his professionalism? Are there not circumstances where written aims and avowals can be as much a hindrance as a help? The political analogy is useful here; both curriculum and political problems are defined within an idiomatic activity, and are uncertain, practical problems.[5] I have remarked earlier that by not writing down the British constitution, it can be argued that our affairs can be better ordered by an appeal to what is left implicit. If we turn to political parties, we might note that the Labour Party's written constitution has been a source of endless acrimony since the 1940s. It is interesting to see that in 1981, the new Social Democratic Party established its 'platform' not with a statement of aims, but with a list of 'Twelve Tasks'. It may well be that in reshaping their curriculum, schools would find it easier to secure a common platform of beliefs not by the laborious and unprofitable exercise of writing down aims, but by agreeing on tasks to be tackled. The values of the new curriculum would, of course, be enshrined within the tasks, but without undue rhetoric or confusing detail.

The technocratic model of curriculum change

But it must be recognised that the urge to write down aims is hard to resist. Nottinghamshire LEA, for example, in a statement on curriculum and policy and staffing from its 'Education policy and standards sub-committee', sets out as a 'principle' that:
Schools should look at:

i   Aims and objectives – what is the purpose of a curriculum?
ii Content – what subject matter is to be used?
iii Methods – what learning experiences and school
    organisation are to be provided?
iv Evaluation – how are the results to be assessed?

It is particularly sad that in the Schools Council's recent document on whole curriculum planning, *The Practical Curriculum*, this technocratic model of change is very much to the fore. Several pages are devoted to elaborations of the Warnock aims, which are intended to 'provide a basis for self-assessment' and are also commended as 'the best basis for teachers, governors and their local authority to discuss and agree the provision of staff . . . materials and cash'. But, of course, a school may have nobler aims than any other in the authority, yet be profligate in the use it makes of its resources. What matters are not aims, but actions.

Clearly, though, aims are connected with actions. But how are they connected? The model we have been presented with so far assumes that action is a feed-forward process in three stages:

   i aims are defined and refined – the *ends* are fixed;
   ii scientific logic is applied to determining the appropriate *means* to secure these ends;
   iii the action results from applying the means, and can be *evaluated* by comparing the results with the stated aims.

This view of action originates from the work of the philosopher J. S. Mill. It is a form of scientific rationalism which looks temptingly neat and systematic. It leads directly to the separation of means and ends, and to the definition of objectives as more detailed ends-statements derived from aims. Ultimately, it leads to the statement of these objectives in measurable form, based on observed behaviours.[6] This approach to curriculum activity has been exploited with great gusto by behavioural psychologists, mainly in the USA. It is also attractive to other social scientists, because its essentially atomistic view of action lends itself to the definition of different stages and classes within the process. Much social science amounts to little more than the invention of category systems of one kind or other. But the objectives approach is open to a number of objections.[7] A few are:

   i there is no consistent way of defining educational objectives;
   ii defining objectives inhibits the exploratory nature of the teaching/learning process;
   iii the more trivial the outcome, the easier to state the objective;
   iv knowledge cannot be reduced to lists of behaviours.

These objections could be dismissed as academic if the approach worked in practice. But American experience shows that, on the contrary, the application of this technocratic model to schools – which has been the result of the accountability movement in the USA over the last decade – has yielded a more impoverished education than before. And while the test results and the statements of objectives have piled up in school staffrooms and administrators' offices, so also has the amount of bureaucracy needed to fuel the system.

What this approach drives out is the craft and intuition upon which imaginative teaching depends. The error arises from the fundamental step of separating means and ends – of believing that aims lead to objectives, and so to means. The modern philosopher Michael Oakeshott has argued that Mill's view of rational action is at fault, because the actions of the politician, the cook, the carpenter and the teacher cannot be split up into objectives, means and evaluation.[8] Oakeshott argues that the *idiom of the activity* constitutes a whole – that our attempt to define *procedures* which describe the activity can never be more than a gross abridgment of the activity, which is characterised by *practical* rather than *technical* knowledge. Knowing the rules an artist follows in painting a picture – knowing what brushes, what canvas he uses – can tell us nothing about how he actually produces the picture itself: unless, of course, the picture has been reduced to areas and numbers.

The danger of the objectives approach is precisely that it reduces teaching to 'painting by numbers'. And it is no coincidence that Mill was a utilitarian philosopher. The whole apparatus of aims – objectives – resources – evaluation appeals to those latter-day utilitarians who so obviously influenced the DES Green Paper of 1977, and whose heavy hand lies not only on subsequent HMI and DES documents, but also on the Schools Council's booklet. Talk of evaluation and 'self-evaluation' is unhelpful, because it is only the *technical* aspects of teaching that can be evaluated. What really matters – the *practical* aspects – is inseparable from the action itself, and can only be judged as an implicit part of the action. We learn, in other words, by doing. All forms of evaluation are reductionist, and therefore distort what they seek to assess.[9]

An alternative view: the arts of deliberation

Oakeshott's view requires that we see ends and means not as separable, but as interacting. And his interpretation of action echoes Aristotle's distinction between the theoretical and the practical. The American educationist Joseph Schwab has adopted a similar view in his paper 'The practical: a language for curriculum'; the title indicates the stance.[10]

What, then, is the value of aims? I would say their value is not to yield specific objectives: this is to misconceive the way we do things and traduce the whole purpose of aims. Aims guide judgment in uncertain situations by informing action. We cannot deduce precise objectives before the action; the whole notion of technocratic planning by objectives applies *ex post hoc* logic to events which have already occurred. The essence of aims is that they must be kept broad so as not to circumscribe choice within action. To make them ever more detailed is to miss the point and go up a cul de sac.

In Schwab's view, the key activity in curriculum planning is *deliberation*. Space does not allow a detailed discussion, but the reader is referred to the noted sources.[11] This extract from Schwab's paper will convey the gist of it:

> Deliberation is complex and arduous. It treats both ends and means and must treat them as mutually determining one another. It must try to identify, with respect to both, what facts may be relevant. . . . It must generate alternative solutions. It must make every effort to trace the branching pathways of consequences which may flow from each alternative and affect desiderata. It must then weigh alternatives and their costs and consequences against one another, and choose, not the *right* alternative, but the *best* one.

The HMI and DES documents lay too much stress on principles and rules, and hence on some concept of *right action*. The right can be the enemy of the good, and does not help in solving practical problems. The slow progress reported in *Curriculum 11–16: A Review of Progress* stems, I think, from this cause. What is important in curriculum development – in my experience – is tools, not rules. My understanding of curriculum planning is of a process made up of human actions to which the methods of physical science seem alien. Schwab's view seems preferable to that of the managerialists and technocrats.

I have devoted some space to this matter since it is, quite simply, of fundamental importance. It not only affects our view of action: it also affects our idea of what education should be about. For it sets aside procedure in order to examine the moral nature of the practical questions by which curriculum is resolved. We are again led back to Aristotle's concept of liberal education, and the error of attempting to design a curriculum around a theoretical principle for its own sake. The approach of Hirst is vulnerable to this charge, being derived from a categorisation of knowledge in terms of logical distinctions between the categories. This is not to say that such a categorisation is of no value; only that, in applying it to curriculum design, it must be seen as secondary to the practical problems of making the curriculum work. And these must be resolved by the arts of deliberation.

The case study of Sheredes School in Chapter 3 makes clear that although the curriculum design drew on Hirst's forms of knowledge and understanding, they were secondary to the solution of practical problems.[12] Geography, for example, is a mandatory element in the 11–16 humanities programme, but is not a distinct form in Hirst's terms. It was included because, in harness with English, history and religious education, the staff were convinced it would be a way of offering a valuable range of experiences which would go beyond the content and objectives of geography for its own sake.

It is important to stress that the deliberative approach is not limited to piecemeal change: indeed, whole curriculum planning may require substantial change (see, for example, the case study of Berkeley Vale School in Chapter 3). The point is that change, in whatever form, must be rooted in practical reasoning and a particular institutional context. Moreover, the deliberative approach is not a free-floating method, lacking moral commitment or rationale: on the contrary, it stems from a distinctive view of liberal education and the moral obligation to offer all pupils a defensibly good education. It does, however, accept that liberal education is inseparable from the resolution of ambiguities, and here it differs quite fundamentally from the view of secondary education which became established in English public schools in the last century, and was then passed (through Morant's 1904 Regulations for Secondary Schools) to the maintained grammar schools and hence to present-day comprehensives. It is essentially a top-down model of education: what is to be taught in secondary schools is to be derived from university entrance requirements, which continue (*pace* Robbins) mainly to be expressed by subject departments in subject terms. So it is that the English sixth form is indistinguishable in its essentials from that in Thomas Arnold's Rugby, and continues to determine the content and form of the 14–16 curriculum and, in some schools, even influences the curriculum in the first three years. What is argued here is instead a bottom-up model, which takes as its starting point where pupils are at the moment, and seeks to bring them inside key aspects of the culture by identifying worthwhile experiences and developing ways of operationalising them. It is an excellent sign that the Cockcroft Report (1982) talks of the need to adopt a bottom-up model for the teaching of mathematics. The deliberative approach to curriculum planning amounts precisely to a set of beliefs and methods by which such a model can be articulated and implemented.

An understanding of how distinctive kinds of cultural experience might be mapped out is a part of this approach, and I shall now look at this more closely.

Developing content areas

Here we come to a grave weakness in the HMI approach to whole curriculum planning, which rests on the eight areas of experience in *Curriculum 11–16*. The similarity of these to Hirst's forms – and their intellectually defective presentation, compared with that of the original – have been noted in Chapter 1. But more serious is the way in which the 'checklist' of the eight areas has come to be seen as the primary instrument of curriculum planning. We learn from *A Review of Progress* that 'In the minds of many heads and teachers it had been a "powerful analytical tool" . . . it had provided "a starting point . . . ".' Others have recommended that subject teachers be given a list of the eight areas, and asked to distribute ten points between them, according to the extent to which their subject contributes to each of the eight areas.[13] These can then be aggregated, and used to express the degree of 'balance' in the curriculum.

Quantitative devices of this sort are evidently quite inappropriate to value judgments: what does it mean to indicate that music contributes twice as much to 'the linguistic' as to 'the ethical'? They also misconstrue the relation between subjects and the whole curriculum. What matters is not the extent to which subjects contribute to areas of knowledge and experience, but how the areas of knowledge and experience can be exploited and interpreted while making use of relevant subjects. The starting point is wrong. But because the Red Book has nothing to say about the interpretation of its eight areas, teachers and administrators may be forgiven for struggling to make sense of an inadequately expressed idea.

One result of this lack of clarity is that the expressive component in the common curriculum – particularly music and drama, but to some extent art and the expressive aspects of English as well – may be neglected in some new schemes. *The School Curriculum* vaguely suggests that pupils 'should retain opportunities for some practical and some aesthetic activity'. In practice, this can mean a choice between art, craft and technical subjects along with music and perhaps drama: and only one subject will be chosen. For example, the Nottinghamshire document referred to above recommends that, in years 4 and 5, the curriculum 'can also be expected to include . . . a practical/creative subject (such as music, art craft or home economics)'. Similarly, the Cheshire LEA 'Working Party on Teacher Staffing Levels in Secondary Schools' (March 1980) uses a curriculum model devised by the 'Cheshire Curriculum Reappraisal Group (CCRAG)', and this shows a single allocation to the 'creative/aesthetic' area in years 4 and 5. This model may be summarised as in Table 2.1:

TABLE 2.1

	Years 1–3	Years 4 and 5	
Linguistic	12.5	12.5	
Mathematical	12.5	12.5	
Ethical/Spiritual	5	5	
Physical	10	5	
Modern Language	10	(0–20)	
Social/Political	15	10	
Creative/Aesthetic	20	10	
Scientific	15	10	
	100%	65%	
Elective courses		20	(12 groups in a 6 fe school: 2 compulsory choices including a modern language if required)
Flexibility time		15	(9 groups: careers, link courses, work experience, possibly 1 exam course)
		100%	

The influence of the Red Book 'checklist' is very apparent. It is therefore interesting to look at a different way of setting out key areas of cultural experience.

Exercise 3: the Australian core curriculum model

The nine 'areas of knowledge and experience' given below are taken from the document *Core Curriculum for Australian Schools*, Curriculum Development Centre, Canberra (1980):[14]

1   *Arts and Crafts*: Arts and crafts cover a wide and diverse area including literature, music, visual arts, drama, wood, metal and plastic crafts, and many others. Whilst in some respects it is not satisfactory to group these together, in the school setting

71

they have many features in common, especially in regard to the techniques and tools used and the approaches adopted towards the shaping and manipulation of materials. The neglect of particular art forms, divided opinions about the need for general aesthetic education as distinct from expression through the arts, and the uneven approach to basic craft teaching in many schools, suggest the need for a comprehensive review of these areas of the curriculum. We have yet to define essential elements of experience, understanding, appreciation and skill, and to select a manageable array of learnings for schools. Until this is done and strong rationales produced, there will be a tendency on the one hand to multiply options and on the other to treat the arts as dispensable in schooling when other pressures obtrude. In fact, they represent major, fundamental forms of human expression, understanding, appreciation and communication. Given the range and diversity of arts and crafts, further studies are needed on the selection, organisation and direction of a sequential core program through all the years of schooling.

2 *Environmental Studies*: The central purpose of environmental studies within the core is awareness and understanding of both the physical and man-made environments and sensitivity to the forces that sustain or may destroy them. This requires both systematic knowledge drawn from such disciplines as biology, geography, landscape architecture, economics, etc., and a readiness by schools to participate in environmental maintenance projects which give students practical experience in the field. As in other areas of the core, there is an emphasis on social action – environmental studies represents a blend of theory and practice which may be organised in many different ways. Within the core, what is important is not the particular kind of organisation, but the environmentalist approach or perspective. This is an amalgam of types of knowledge and understanding, and a disposition to sustain and protect the environment.

3 *Mathematical Skills and Reasoning and their Application*: In addition to an understanding of basic number processes and their application in individual and social life, the main role of mathematics within the core is as a form of symbolising and quantifying. Mathematics contributes to a view of the world, not merely practical skills, and this view needs to be fostered through problem-solving approaches, a wide range of

applications and the training of reasoning. Applied mathematics relates to several other subject areas, for example, sciences, social sciences and some aspects of craft and technology. The relevance of mathematics to contemporary life has become increasingly apparent through calculators, computers and other technical applications, of which students need at least a general understanding.

4 *Social, Cultural and Civic Studies*: The focus of social, cultural and civic studies is the understanding of what is required for effective participation in social life, including the major political, social and cultural institutions and processes of Australia as a democratic and economically advanced society. These studies include consideration of the place and significance of belief and value systems (religion, ideology) in our society. They have dimensions which are both historical (social/political/economic history) and contemporary (social issues and trends, the law, consumerism, social values, etc.). They may be taught separately as 'social sciences' (including history, economics, etc.) and 'cultural studies' (including religion and values education), or in an integrated fashion. The scope of these studies should include the diverse sub-cultures and common cultures within Australia (including ethnic and Aboriginal sub-cultures), and in other societies, and the ideas of an international or world order. Opportunity should be provided for students to appraise and assess the evolution, present status of and trends in the social and civic order and to undertake practical action projects. As prospective citizens, students have a part to play in deciding the future of their country and of the international order. For these studies to have practical relevance they must relate to the present life experiences and interests of the students.

5 *Health Education*: Growing public concern over health standards of Australians, reflecting the economic and psychic costs of ill-health, and the introduction of extensive and costly community health programs, suggest a need for sustained effort in school education. Health education has an immediate value and an impact on students which are available to few other areas of the curriculum.

The core curriculum needs to give scope to physical, emotional, mental and community health studies, and to provide opportunity for practical applications. 'Health', in becoming a school subject, may run the risk of being perceived

73

as yet another body of knowledge to be known about rather than directly experienced. The health area needs to be approached through a wide range of studies ranging from the sciences of human biology and nutrition to programmes of sport and physical recreation, general health care and relaxation. As with arts and crafts, there is need for an overall review of the area, to produce a well-organised practical framework for teaching and to gain acceptance of the need for all students to become involved in self-help health education programmes.

6   *Scientific and Technological Ways of Knowing and their Social Applications*: Science and technology are fundamental forms of human thought and powerful applications of organised problem-solving to practical situations in the everyday life of individuals, for whole societies and for the world order. They exemplify not only rational but also intuitive, imaginative and creative powers of the highest order. They are decisive forces in the transformation of social and economic life, belief systems and working life. Their study in the core requires an emphasis on forms of knowledge, synthesis, interpretation and extrapolation of data, problem-solving, decision-making, theory–practice relations and social action. They are a means of interpreting and modifying the environment. Thus, scientific and technological studies need to pay attention to social issues, inter-relationships among science, technology and social trends and needs, and the historical conditions giving rise to scientific and technological change. Although choice of material for learning may vary widely, science and technology in the core should provide opportunity for a common set of skills, understandings and dispositions – scientific and technical thinking and their applications.

7   *Communication*: Communication includes both verbal and non-verbal modes and relates equally to knowledge and feeling – and these frequently interact, as for example in face-to-face conversation. We must select for the core those which are basic and essential. Language studies are an indispensable tool in many areas of learning and are intimately related to student thinking and expression. They include listening, speaking, reading and writing, which should be kept in balance throughout the school years. Non-verbal communication is equally a fundamental part of social life. Visual learning directs students towards an understanding and appraisal of the mass-media and visual competence is necessary in many school subjects. Body

communication, apart from its significance in everyday life, has a central place in several of the arts. Should the core include languages other than English? Despite the persuasive arguments advanced for foreign and 'ethnic' languages, it would be difficult at present to justify these as part of a *practical* core for all students. What is indisputably essential is that all Australians should become competent users of the English language. How far the *core* should and could extend to include any language other than English is a question over which educators are divided and the Centre would wish to have more discussion – and evidence – on this point.

8   *Moral Reasoning and Action, Value and Belief Systems*: The development of morality and the capacity to discriminate amongst values and beliefs is both a crucial part of the overall development of the rounded person and a civic necessity. Transformation of moral action from the level of habitual and routine behaviour in childhood to a mature stage of critical analysis and reflective action requires a systematic, continuing approach throughout the years of schooling. Values education relates to many aspects of life in addition to moral behaviour, but has close affinities with it. Whilst the teaching of morality and values, as such, readily lends itself to abuse through indoctrination, its neglect in the curriculum may be regarded as a serious deficiency in many schools. The teaching of morality and values need not, and perhaps ought not, to depend on a separate course, but may be incorporated in other areas – for example social, cultural and civic studies or the arts – and within established subjects and in a wide range of school relationships between students and teachers. Whilst the teaching of religious belief and practice cannot claim a place in a core, teaching *about* religion may be regarded as essential for all students in developing their understanding of the world in which they live.

9   *Work, Leisure and Lifestyle*: The notion of educating for present and future life is of central importance in schooling. Whilst all other core areas should contribute to this, there remain a number of aspects of universal experience which may not be touched upon at all unless some additional, umbrella-like area is included in the core curriculum. There is much debate about the extent to which schools as distinct from other social agencies or indeed individuals themselves should shoulder responsibility for 'education for life'. The case is complex, and

cannot be argued here. The Centre accepts that for many different reasons schools ought to incorporate into the core curriculum a progressive introduction to the working environment, to developing and changing human relationships, to leisure time interests and pursuits, and to such universal requirements of our culture as the ability to drive a car, plan a budget, keep records, purchase goods wisely, and organise a household. Entire curricula have been built around such a 'life preparation' notion but the weakness of this approach has been shown to be a neglect of the fundamental forms of human knowledge and experience, and of the skills required to participate in them. It seems preferable, therefore, to build a life preparation element into the core, to plan it around a selection of requirements of everyday life, and teach it at the levels of knowledge, understanding and reflective practice rather than low-level skills and techniques.

This extract has been given in full because there are probably more similarities than differences between British and Australian culture, yet there are few evident similarities between the two lists of key areas, nor between the way they are explained. The Australian list not only outlines content and concepts, but also indicates where there is uncertainty or even conflict. And in some respects (e.g. multi-cultural education) the Australians may have confronted issues which we have yet to tackle. The following questions point to some interesting points of difference:

1 'Arts and crafts' include both creative and expressive subjects, as in the HMI Red Book. What might link drama or music with metalwork or design? Does this seem the most practical way of incorporating these subjects? Might drama and music be more effectively interrelated with other subjects?

2 How might 'the environmentalist approach' be made part of other curriculum areas? Is this aspect of our culture present in the HMI/DES lists?

3 How does mathematics contribute 'a view of the world'? Does conventional school mathematics present such a view?

4 Does the category 'Social, cultural and civic studies' correspond to any of the eight HMI areas of experiences? Does it correspond at all to the faculty of 'humanities' as an 11–16 core element, as taught in some schools?

5 Compare the DES treatment of physical education with that

here of 'health education'. Which seems to justify itself more convincingly in educational terms?

6 'Science and technology' are treated in similar terms. But does technology use the same concepts and methods as science? How different is a physicist from an engineer?

7 'Scientific and technological studies need to pay attention to social issues'. Is there a danger of teaching *about* science, rather than teaching science? Should the implications of science and technology be a matter for another area – e.g. 4 or 8?

8 Compare the treatment of foreign languages in 'Communication' with that in *The School Curriculum*. Is there a case for making a foreign language part of the core in the UK? Which could it be?

9 How are multi-cultural issues dealt with in areas 4 and 7? How should these be related to the core curriculum?

10 Examine the position of religious education as set out in area 8, and compare it with its place in *The School Curriculum*. Should we teach *about* religion, rather than religion itself?

11 Have there been proposals in the UK for curricula built around the notion of 'life preparation', as discussed in area 9? How far should these matters figure in the core?

Comments on questions

1 Attempts in some English schools to link art or craft with music or drama do not seem to have been notably satisfactory. The reason may be that the expressive aspect of music and drama – which enables them to lead us to knowledge of ourselves, and of others – is less strongly marked in techno-aesthetic subjects like art and craft.

2 There is scant reference to the environment in the British publications. Yet our island is much smaller than the Australian continent. It can, though, be made an aspect of work in humanities and creative areas of a core curriculum – and in science, too.

3 The Cockcroft Report (1982) reflects the uncertainty mathematicians have about the philosophy of their subject. Most school mathematics is still routine skills. But modern mathematics in particular can be taught to bring out the way in which patterns are identified and then expressed in numerical or symbolic forms by means of notation. What kind of mathematics should be part of the core?

77

4   This category – as elaborated in the Australian document – seems very similar to the notion of a humanities faculty. But there is no direct equivalent in the eight 'areas of experience', and although 'humanities' is mentioned as an aspect of the core in *The School Curriculum*, there is no attempt to discuss what it might involve. At this point the curriculum planner needs firmer ground: Hirst's forms of knowledge and understanding are the kind of analysis which can be helpful. Instead, the HMI and DES begin to talk about 'personal and social development', which is such a general term – in many ways, a synonym for education itself – that the discussion is not advanced very much.

5   The DES treatment of physical education is sketchy, and assumes it is a good thing. But what effect does school Pe really have on post-school life styles? This discussion of how to justify Pe in the core seems timely.

6   I have doubts about the wisdom of lumping science and technology together in school curriculum design. 'Technology' does, of course, apply science to practical problems; but if it is given this emphasis in school, it is swamped by hardware (like control systems, or electronics, or engines) and becomes costly and teacher-centred. The term is broad enough to apply to applied arts as well, and in my experience makes an ideal focus for a 'design' course in the techno-aesthetic area. Designing the interior of a caravan – or, for that matter, a pottery teapot – involves both aesthetic and technological considerations, and is more accessible to pupils than elaborate apparatus and machines.

7   There is an important point to debate here. If the purpose of science in the core curriculum is – as it might be – to initiate pupils into the nature of scientific thought and method, discussion of social issues is irrelevant. Yet such discussion must be a part of the core experience. SCISP is an example of a programme which seeks to do both things, and the solution will probably be some similar sort of compromise. But such discussion ought not to be omitted from the humanities, either: technology has had an important effect on the course of history, but often gets no detailed treatment.

8   It can be argued – and some linguists would choose to – that there is no *educational* case for putting a foreign language in the 11–16 core. But all pupils ought to experience some foreign tongue 11–13, so that they can thereafter make a sensible choice. Some schools offer a rotation scheme for, say, French and German in years 1–3. But is there then enough experience for the pupil's choice to be well informed? It is worth adding that in some

American cities, Latin has been added to the 11–13 core for all pupils, with interesting results. 'The purpose is to help pupils, especially the lowest achieving ones in inner-city schools, improve their English language skills . . . the project was successful in improving the reading vocabulary and comprehension scores of target students by more than one month for each month of instruction.'[15] There may be a better educational case for core Latin than for core French! Not, though, for its own sake (e.g. for abler pupils) but as a means to another end. There may, of course, be a *political* case for making French a core language – and the DES statement hints at this (apropos our membership of the EEC). But is the school the best place to teach it? Surely motivation is what matters? Money might be better spent on adult language skill centres. The introduction of graded tests in school French teaching is a way of boosting motivation. But by stressing testable skills, it undermines claims for the educational benefits of language teaching. And the big question remains: if a foreign language is taking up 10 per cent or so of the 11–16 core, what is being displaced to make room for it? What does language teaching offer which will help the pupil acquire practical and intellectual autonomy for adult life?

9   There has been considerable discussion in Australia about the place of multi-cultural studies in core curriculum. The principal author of the Australian document (M. Skilbeck) has written.[16]

> The effect of the Centre's approach to core curriculum is to challenge what we believe is an excessively narrow focus in recent Australian discussions . . . and to suggest that we need to appreciate that ethnic identity and diversity and the specific learning needs of ethnic groups constitute but one dimension of multiculturalism. . . . Core curriculum analysis addresses itself to the dimensions . . . of common culture and sets as an educational programme not the reproduction or amplification of particular cultural subsets of our society but the fostering and indeed creation of new cultural orders which will incorporate but transcend existing categories – ethnic and others.

There is, in short, a danger that what has been termed 'the race relations industry' will, by exaggerating ethnic differences, do these groups a disservice: a common curriculum must reflect society, and act as a melting pot from which a new synthesis is made. Unless this is done for all pupils – regardless of their ethnic group – they will not be able to act as autonomous persons in the national culture.

10   It can be argued that religion is caught and not taught. The essence of it is a religious experience, and places of worship are built and consecrated to celebrate and foster these experiences. Can this be done in school classrooms? Is it, indeed, the business of schools to do such things? The American constitution explicitly bans them. On the other hand, there is an equally strong case for ensuring that the differing natures of religious belief, and their influence on man and his world, should be a component of the core curriculum. It does not follow, though, that this is best done through Re as a separate slot on the timetable.[17] It may be better done in association with a humanities core element.

11   There have been such proposals. One emerged from the Educational Priority Area experiment in Liverpool, and has been heavily criticised for limiting the horizons of working-class pupils. But some have seen it as helpful in attempts to flesh out the rather tenuous concept of 'community education'. More recently, a number of bodies including the Manpower Services Commission have become involved with a proposal to provide schoolchildren with 'Skills for Working Life', and the Secretary of State for Education, Sir Keith Joseph, declared at the 1981 Conservative Party Conference that the 14–16 school years should more closely reflect the world of work. This trend towards vocationalism occurred in the USA when economic conditions grew harsher, but it has had no beneficial effects.[18] On the contrary, by stressing particular 'skills' at the expense of 'fundamental forms of human knowledge and experience' (to quote the Australian document), it leads to an impoverished curriculum which is bad for pupil and for society alike.

The above exercise has drawn attention to a number of important issues. Fundamental to the argument is the way in which our culture can be analysed and converted to curriculum experience. I find the Australian statement an admirably honest attempt to tackle issues which are sidestepped in the DES and HMI publications. Only by airing them and looking critically at them will we become better at solving curriculum problems.

A central problem is to agree on what should be put into the core, and what can safely be left out. The next exercise begins with a clearly written recommendation on core curriculum by another LEA, and then pursues the idea of mandatory core subjects by looking at some specific curriculum areas:

Exercise 4: Content and process in core curriculum

Here is an extract from the *ILEA Statement on the curriculum for pupils aged 5 to 16* (March 1981, Inner London Education Authority):

Characteristics of good practice: recommendations for curriculum planning

There are many approaches to establishing the general principles on which curriculum planning may be based. One example is that used by HMI in the document 'Curriculum 11–16', based on identifying eight areas of experience to which pupils should have access. The approach adopted here is to suggest principles broadly based on defining the skills and knowledge and attitudes children need to acquire in order to develop as individuals and members of society, and correspondingly the learning experiences the school should provide. Two general points must be made before these principles are stated; these relate to equality of opportunity for the sexes and to multi-ethnic education. Curriculum opportunities in the mixed secondary school must be open equally to boys and girls and in single sex schools staff should do all they can to make available to their pupils the curriculum opportunities that would be offered to pupils in schools for the opposite sex. This is specially important in mathematics and physical sciences for girls. In planning their curriculum the staff of all schools should constantly bear in mind the need to prepare pupils for a multi-ethnic society.

The suggested principles are as follows:
   (i) Children must have the freedom to play a major part in determining their own future lives. This necessitates learning enough to be in a position to exercise some choice. Thus, schools must provide conditions for girls and boys to learn and to learn how to learn. Entailed by this is work in the use of the English language, speaking, listening, reading and writing in all areas of the curriculum, not merely in lessons labelled English on the timetable. It presupposes understanding to some degree mathematical ways of thinking and some ability to handle numbers. It implies the introduction of careers education.
   (ii) All societies have regarded it as proper that the new generation shall learn something of whence they came,

of how mankind had developed, of the history of their own civilisation and others, and of man in his contemporary environment. Thus, the curriculum will include, in some form or other, biology, history, geography, even if they be called ecological, social or environmental studies.

(iii) Children need to share in the knowledge of ways in which we have learned partly to understand nature and to control it for good or ill. This is valuable in itself and economically essential in a technological society. It follows that there should be some science and technology for all.

(iv) All pupils need access to the arts, including drama, music and the visual arts.

(v) All pupils should experience the self-respect and confidence that come from a degree of mastery of some practical skill. This will, in its wider applications, go beyond mere mechanical efficiency.

(vi) All must be aware that they ought to contribute to society if they have to draw upon it; that each must contribute what he can and must value the contribution of others. The curriculum should therefore include religious education and provide opportunities for moral, social and political education.

(vii) While English is, indeed, a major world language, it is helpful to study a foreign language and the country where it is spoken, even if that study be not carried to the point of mastery of grammar.

(viii) Physical and health education have a necessary place in promoting a full enjoyment and appreciation of life; this is important for all, including the handicapped and the delicate.

In considering the curriculum of a secondary school the inspectorate would expect to find that a broad and balanced curriculum was being offered to pupils, based on an agreed set of aims derived from a considered philosophy of the curriculum. In particular, it would expect that the study of English, mathematics, science and religious and physical education in some form would be continued throughout the years from 11 to 16. It would expect that pupils would normally be given an opportunity of studying a foreign language for at least two years between the ages of 11 to 16 and for a longer period if they wished. It would expect each pupil's programme normally to include for the whole secondary course an arts/craft element and a component from the group of subjects including geography, history and social/environmental studies. It would expect to see careers education and preparation for the world of work starting in the third year and continuing through the fourth and fifth years.

Health education (principle viii) generally includes sex education. A view of this was given by Mary Warnock in her 'Personal Column' in *The Times Educational Supplement* of 19 December 1980:

> Katharine Whitehorn writing about sex education in *The Observer*, November 16, said this: 'If the moralists really want the kids to grow up in ignorance, I'd say insistence on sex being taught as a subject in schools was much the best way to go about it. Then it would be just one more dead tedious thing for teachers to drone on about.'
>
> Without wishing to enter (yet) any controversy about sex education, I must say how deeply right I think she is. Being taught things at school normally turns the subject matter into something not only dead but unreal. Efforts to be up-to-date, or to relate the subject to the child's experience have little effect.
>
> The only result is that more is sucked in to the death chamber. The moment something is a school subject, particularly if it is compulsory, then it is inevitably connected with the yawning, aching boredom of the classroom. Never since school have I myself suffered such physical agonies of boredom as I remember when learning, for example, about tea or rice or other vaguely 'geographical' topics.

It is generally assumed that most people, and particularly scientists themselves, are in favour of more science in the core curriculum. But this is not necessarily the case. The issue of *Education* for 3 July 1981 carried this item:

> The Government is to issue a consultative paper on teaching science before the end of the year which is likely to propose that no pupil should be able to drop science altogether while at school, or to study only one of the common science subjects. The document was promised by Lady Young, Minister of State at the Department, when she addressed a London University Institute of Education HMI conference on science teaching in London on Tuesday. The DES document will be the first phase

of a consultative process announced by Lady Young in April as part of the follow up to *The School Curriculum*.

'It will be concerned with the fundamental question of how we can provide suitable balanced science courses for pupils across the ability range.'

The same conference heard a counter view:

The Minister's views were followed by those of Professor Lewis Elton, head of University of Surrey's Institute for Educational Technology. He proceeded to attack not only the Department's analysis of the science teaching needs of the nation, but the entire Government strategy for economic rejuvenation. He was critical of the belief that scientific success was somehow linked to economic prosperity. During the past 100 years, during which time Britain's scientists had achieved the greatest renown throughout the world, the nation had witnessed a gradual economic decline.

Professor Elton went on to question other shibboleths of science teaching. Again comparing Europe's record with that of Britain, he said 'We ought to question whether money spent on laboratories in schools and universities is well spent.' Schools had tried and failed to get pupils interested in engineering, yet there was never any need to teach accountancy, law or medicine in school to ensure a supply for these professions. The education system was conning children, he said, 'which is a despicable activity'.

At the 1981 meeting of the Association for Science Education there were other critical voices (*Education*, 9 January 1981):

The Government's proposal for a core curriculum to ensure all children learned some science before they left school was attacked as 'dangerous and pernicious nonsense' by Dr. Richard West, director of the University of Sussex school of education. He put forward an alternative curriculum based on the scientific study of the self and the relation of the individual to society and to the environment. It should include the study of self-sufficiency and the means of production, problem-solving and creativity. Science could fit into that kind of coherent philosophy.

The important issue was the attempt to link the school system with the world of work and industry in either its recumbent or resuscitated form. He questioned the naïveté of this approach.

Industry was a de-skilling process that sought a compliant workforce that operated well below its educational level. Education was by definition concerned with change and with making people question. The Government's core curriculum was a recipe for alienation.

The traditional science curriculum, based on the Holy Trinity of physics, chemistry and biology, did not justify a place in the core curriculum: it had outlived its usefulness. 'The close link between school science and the universities legitimates it as a valid subject but it has not one jot to do with the outside world, economic regeneration or the future needs of children as adults and parents.'

The Nuffield and Schools Council projects had defined 'science for all' in meritocratic terms and the publishers and equipment makers – the tinkers and tailors of the system – had supported them to the full. But by the mid-1970s fundamental questions were being asked: did such a curriculum meet the needs of the children? Since an *ad hoc, à la carte* curriculum had failed to deliver the goods, the answer seemed to be to reduce the curriculum to its basics – literacy, numeracy, a foreign language and basic scientific literacy, with a statutory dose of Keep Fit and Keep Clean.

Apart from questioning the kind of science to be taught in the core curriculum, this also queries the justification of core science in economic terms, and the fashionable link between school and work. This link is explicit in the following extract (*Education*, 3 July 1981):

The Schools Council Convocation endorsed an ambitious 18-point plan on Tuesday as the basis for the Council's future policy on the 16 to 19 year olds. Central to the master plan was the idea of 'education for capability' – an attempt to give a strong shift to the curriculum from academic knowledge towards skills, including 'social and life skills'.

Also included in the plan were: work experience for all students, including the most able; new mixes of part-time school and employment; use of distance learning techniques; developing profile reports; and broadening the sixth-form syllabus through Intermediate level exams. Below the age of 16 the Council intends to intensify work on the Industry and Skills for Employment projects.

Amplifying their plan afterwards, Council secretary Mr. John

Mann thought all school subjects should be reorientated towards the practical.

'Education for Capability' was the title of an advertisement bearing a number of signatories (including the Schools Council's secretary and chairman) which appeared during March 1981, and offered the following rationale:

> We, the undernamed, believe that there is a serious imbalance in Britain today in the full process which is described by the two words 'education' and 'training'. Thus, the idea of the 'educated man' is that of a scholarly, leisured individual who has been neither educated nor trained to exercise useful skills. Those who study in secondary schools or higher education increasingly specialise; and normally in a way which means that they are taught to practise only the skills of scholarship and science; to understand but not to act. They gain knowledge of a particular area of study, but not ways of thinking and working which are appropriate for use outside the education system.
>
> We believe that this imbalance is harmful to individuals, to industry and to society. Individual satisfaction stems from doing a job well through the exercise of personal capability. Acquisition of this capability is inhibited by the present system of education which stresses the importance of analysis, criticism and the acquisition of knowledge and generally neglects the formulation and solution of problems, doing, making and organising; in fact, constructive and creative activity of all sorts.
>
> The resolution of this problem in Britain has been vitiated by discussing it in terms of two cultures: the arts and the sciences. It is significant that we have no word for the culture that the Germans describe as 'Technik' or the mode of working that the French describe as a 'Metier'.
>
> We consider that there exists in its own right a culture which is concerned with doing, making and organising. This culture emphasises craftsmanship and the making of useful artefacts; the design, manufacture and marketing of goods and services; specialist occupations with an active mode of work; the creative arts; and the day to day management of affairs.
>
> We believe that education should spend more time in teaching people skills and preparing them for life outside the education system; and that the country would benefit significantly in economic terms from this re-balancing towards education for capability.

The emphasis on 'skills' is evident in *The Practical Curriculum*, and also in the HMI Primary Survey (1978). Apropos the latter, R. Dearden has written (in C. Richards (ed.) (1980), *The Primary Curriculum*, London, A. & C. Black):

> Intellectual development (throughout the report) is thought of as a developing of certain apparently quite general *skills*. . . . This conception . . . is, to put it mildly, highly controversial. . . . Can there be such general skills as skill in noticing, observing skill, thinking skill, comprehension skill or listening skill? . . . Where there is generality, then let us by all means draw attention to it and so anticipate whole classes of future experiences; but at the same time let us also recognise that 'skills' can become a mindless incantation serving only to render vague what we should be seeking to teach.

The above extracts have deliberately been taken from everyday sources rather than academic publications, to illustrate the way in which teachers can encounter core curriculum issues and reflect professionally upon them as part of their normal business. Yet some important issues are raised here:

1 Compare the ILEA 'suggested principles' with *Curriculum 11–16*. Note that (iv) and (v) make a distinction between the expressive and the practical. Does the Red Book do this?

2 Is it true that 'Being taught things at school normally turns the subject matter into something not only dead but unreal', as Mary Warnock asserts? Is this an argument for inquiry-based learning? Or, at any rate, for the importance in the common curriculum of *how* the core is taught, as well as of *what* is taught?

3 Why should science be a core subject? Does science 'train the mind'? Is it because adults who have not been taught science will feel alienated from a scientific environment? Or does conventional school science itself alienate pupils (as Richard West suggests)? Is science a necessary core element because industry needs scientists and engineers? Who should decide on the core: the providers or the users?

4 Should 'education spend more time in teaching people skills' (Education for Capability)? What is the difference between 'knowledge' and 'ways of thinking and working'?

Comments on questions

1 The ILEA statement seems in many ways an improvement on both the Red Book and *The School Curriculum*: it is unpretentious, but advances a concisely expressed, liberal view.

2 The HMI secondary survey reinforces the impression that although, since the Bullock report, many schools have allocated more time to English than ever before, most pupils find it more boring than it seemed to be in the pre-Bullock 1960s, when the doctrines were less prescriptive and the feeling more liberal.[19] Regarding subjects as important does not make them interesting. What matters is the attitude with which staff approach the whole curriculum. Recipes and committee recommendations can inhibit the imagination on which good teaching depends.

3 Most school science – as the HMI secondary survey bears out – is what Schwab termed (in 1963) 'a rhetoric of conclusions'. Purveying facts and going through bogus experiments to 'discover' them is a form of anti-science. The philosophy of science – and its history – are almost completely neglected: yet they show so plainly that real science is not about things, but about people. The issue is doubly important, not only because of DES pressure to make science a core subject, but also because of current discussion about integrated or unified science.[20] SCISP remains the only substantial course available 13–16, and is a far-sighted and commendable piece of work under the Schools Council's aegis. But it has faults: it is based too naively on one particular psychological theory of learning, and succeeds perhaps in spite of its detailed catechism of objectives rather than because of them. Skilled teachers learn how to treat these as guidelines, and how to use the material to their own ends. New unified courses are urgently needed, and must offer worthwhile core experiences not only to those continuing with science post-16, but also to those with no sustained commitment to science.

4 The talk of 'skills' is partly a sign of growing awareness that the curriculum really must be broader, and have a form appropriate to comprehensive schooling for all. People are beginning to realise that there is a great deal of knowledge around, so some sort of 'instant learning pack' is going to be handy. At the same time, the stress on inert knowledge for the sake of examination success – the 'key facts' view of education – purveyed by traditional grammar schools, is seen to be irrelevant and futile. The 'Education for Capability' lobby seems to have added these two responses together, and concluded that the right recipe is to give up

knowledge and go for skills: especially the skills of 'doing, making and organising'.

This is well-intentioned but muddled. It is certainly true that propositional knowledge of an often valueless kind is pursued in the grammar school curriculum: the HMI secondary survey provides the evidence. It is also true that this same 'academic' view of schooling has, for over a century, reduced even science teaching to examinable facts and off-the-peg solutions, and thus excluded genuine scientific inquiry and reflection. It has also encouraged the view that practical activity – as opposed to writing – is for second-rate minds. All this is deplorable. But it is simple-minded to suppose that 'skills' exist in isolation from knowledge, and in some magic way convey the essence without the factual content. Most skills are heavily dependent on facts. If I do not know, as an amateur plasterer, that one should begin at the top of a patch rather than the bottom, I will not be much good at it. Indeed, the magazine *Which?* has given a description of plastering in words and pictures: the 'skill' has been expressed as knowledge. The line between propositional and procedural knowledge – as between facts and skills – is not easily drawn. The person with 'capability' will, once again, be the person who is autonomous – who knows how to make judgments about a range of key aspects of the culture. But autonomy does not come merely from learning general skills – not least because, as Dearden points out, general skills simply do not exist.[21]

Core curriculum issues

The simulation exercise which concludes this chapter gives the reader the opportunity to reason through these matters in the setting of a whole school curriculum. But before reaching this point, I should like to offer brief notes on some issues in curriculum planning which are of particular importance in designing and implementing a core curriculum.

1   Curriculum change as a practical art

How a school begins to re-think its curriculum is much more important than starting out with detailed prescriptions of *what* should be done. I have argued here that the technocratic model which pervades HMI and DES writings is inappropriate for the solution of curriculum problems. Dreaming up grandiose statements of aims and then trying to operationalise them with detailed objectives often leads to much talk and still more paper, but very little change.

The *method* by which complex undertakings are pursued is often seen as incidental to the objectives of the enterprise. Yet it should be remembered that Hermann Bondi has remarked: 'There is no more to science than its method.' And just as scientific method has yielded remarkable results in unravelling the physical world, so we must use an appropriate method for tackling the problems which arise when complex human actions and interactions are under consideration.

Climate is a part of method: the shared values and understandings of an organic community directly promote – or obstruct – change and innovation.[22] The essentially *moral* nature of curriculum problems needs to be brought out from the start. What is in question is not the good of this physics teacher, or that modern languages department, but of the pupils. By posing challenging questions for debate, a school can establish an atmosphere of fraternal questioning and commitment.

The result of this process will be the establishment of a *platform*. The usage comes from that of political parties in defining that corpus of beliefs which – however loosely – bind its members together. The 'broad church' to which a school's staff will belong will establish that corpus of beliefs around some view of education. Once this *theory* of education is agreed upon, it will underpin the decisions that lie ahead. Teachers should not be shy of the word *theory* and confine it to academics in ivory towers: as Popper has argued, some theory must underlie all conscious actions.[23] Education is a practical activity which expresses a theory by the way it is done. Attempts to write down this theory or set of beliefs in the form of elaborate statements of aims should be eschewed. Writing it down will convince nobody. What matters is that the beliefs are implicitly understood, not explicitly committed to paper. Our legalistic society gives too much weight to formal written statements, and too little to the informal contracts which spring up between people who share a common faith in good actions.

It is fashionable to assist the process of determining new curriculum goals by a flight to empiricism: in particular, by 'pupil day studies' in which some teacher or visitor follows a class or pupil around the school. And sometimes heads of departments are asked to appear before staff committees and give accounts of their intentions and organisations.

In some schools these devices may be a necessary preliminary to establishing an awareness that all is not well, so that the climatic shift can begin. But there are a number of dangers. First, it must be recognised that a teacher's perception of what a pupil is experiencing will be quite different from that of the pupil, and that any observer will always distort the process under observation. Second, the value of the data obtained from classroom studies is usually open to interpretation in different ways. Third, it tends to confirm what everyone knows: that this teacher is better than that one, that this department is dull, and so on. Fourth, getting data from classrooms or from departments is very time-consuming and not a little threatening, and may not advance the argument much at all. The result is that initial enthusiasm can give way to dissension. Finally, such exercises imply that the existing structure is taken for granted, since it forms the basis of the inquiry. Fundamental change may thus be rendered more difficult.

It may often be better to let teachers see what is being said about other schools tackling similar problems: Chapter 1 of this book seeks to do this by summarising the HMI surveys and other documents. Some teachers will respond by seeing at once the equivalent weaknesses in their own school: you do not need to take your temperature to be sure you have 'flu. Others will reject the implied analogy, and maintain that their school's option system is all right. The method of *deliberation* will suffice to bring out the truth of the matter. In staff discussions, leading questions will be put and answers will be accepted or challenged. Exercise 1 in Chapter 1 is an attempt to indicate how a deliberative process of this kind might be established.

The case studies in Chapter 3 give examples of core curricula both in established schools and in those starting from scratch. The main advantage enjoyed by the new schools is that the *platform* is much easier to build, because the *climate* can be engendered from the very beginning and gradually reinforced as more staff join. But many new schools have quite traditional curriculums: the fact of a school being new may mean nothing in terms of innovation. The opportunity is there, but it must be seized. The role of the head in promoting change has been widely recognised, but it is probably more climatic than directive. The heads of many innovating schools are not notably assertive or opinionated – often the reverse. But they will have a *vision* – some kind of *theory* – about education and an appropriate curriculum, even though this may be quite inchoate and not readily expressible in terms of explicit aims. It is, however, enough to inspire one or two staff, and thus engender the right climate.

2 Evaluation

This is another fashionable concern. But to see it as a separable part of the business of teaching and learning is to misconceive the nature of curriculum action. The HMI/DES doctrine that written aims and objectives should be used to evaluate the results of school process is bound to lead to a diminished form of curriculum if taken seriously.[24]

This is not, though, to say that schools should not be answerable for what they do, or not render an account of themselves. It is rather to argue that what can be measured and assessed by performance tests is the least important part of what schools are for. The same objection applies to the vogue for 'pupil profiles', which make the extraordinary assertion that a few numbers and comments on a card can reduce an entire personality to a computer entry in some allegedly 'objective' way.

There is evidence that employers are not notably keen to use profiles, and indeed rely mainly – and quite properly – on interviews, with examination results as a kind of back up. Profiles have become popular because of dissatisfaction with traditional forms of 16-plus examination, particularly for less able pupils. But schools which have adopted O level and CSE examinations making use of course work in the assessment find high levels of pupil engagement. The danger is that the current enthusiasm for profiles will lead to the worst of all worlds: traditional O levels for the most able – nourished by a grammar-school curriculum – and profiles for the rest.

Perhaps the most disturbing thing about profiling is its intrusiveness: the traditional examination distances the pupil from an assessment of him, by basing its judgment on an oblique measure of his performance – usually his ability to reach a satisfactory standard in a school subject. But the profile settles for nothing less than the private world of the pupil: his relationships with others, his likes and dislikes. In a confidential reference, these are aspects of his behaviour which might be touched on, but which will be mediated through the referee. In the profile, all is unmasked – or purports to be. But, of course, subjectivity is just as much involved. And in completing the profile, the implication is that a human being can be summarised in a single document.

Regular assessment of pupils must be a part of any core curriculum programme. But it should be based on written statements rather than quantitative measures of 'achievement' and 'effort', and be used not for sorting and grading pupils but as a way of sharing staff knowledge of them, and helping to diagnose learning difficulties and discover aptitudes.[25] Too much attention to the end results of the educational process can divert attention from what really matters – how it is thought about at the beginning. For it is the *intention* which guides the action, and the evaluation which counts is made up of the intrinsic judgments which are an inseparable part of the action itself.

3   Resources for learning

Effective core curriculum teaching requires a variety of learning strategies. Books will be needed in plenty, but so also will worksheets, study guides and other *realia*. At least books will, in general, not be needed in complete sets. It is usually better to have a smaller number but of greater variety.

An offset litho machine will be central to an adequate reprographic facility. But the existence of a resource and reprographic centre is no guarantee of a good curriculum. In the 1970s, a number of new schools were set up around the concept of 'resource-based learning' for its own sake, without any underlying rationale of the curriculum. Often a bizarre concept of staff democracy was stirred into the brew for good measure. The result can easily be muddle, public distrust and expensive equipment broken or unused. And important though democratic decision-making is in formulating a whole curriculum, it must be subordinate to the arts of deliberation and the appropriate distribution of tasks. Effective leadership need not mean unaccountable hierarchies. The effective use of resources will spring from careful discussion in year and faculty teams in an informed and purposive climate. And although worksheets can be tatty and encourage pupil passivity, they can also be vivid and a great enhancement to pupil learning.[26]

Schools without the space for setting up a central resource facility should not see this as a limitation. Local resource areas in faculty spaces, with perhaps a quite small room used as the school reprographic centre, can work every bit as well. What is perhaps more important is some provision of secretarial help for typing staff materials. Ideally a staff secretary should be at least half-time in a six fe school. This may mean looking afresh at the way ancillary staff are deployed, with perhaps less provision in the science and technical areas. This will correspond with new thinking about the whole curriculum, and about the kind of science and kind of CDT work that should be done as part of a core programme.

4 Mixed ability teaching

Adequate discussion of pupil grouping is a lamentable omission from the HMI or DES documents.[27] The HMI paper on MAT makes the error of assuming that there is some unidimensional concept of ability which can be used to allocate pupils into sets or streams. It is dominated by attempts to judge MAT by its *products* – some form of pupil assessment, of which no details are given – rather than to consider the way in which MAT can generate different sorts of learning *processes*. This is a defect the HMI report shares with most of the published research on the subject.[28] For *how* MAT is done reflects the shared values of the staff. If they don't believe in it, it will be badly done. It is therefore an issue directly linked with attitudes to the curriculum. How to group pupils is a curriculum problem.

It is also evidently a moral problem: is it right to differentiate pupils by ability, when the evidence shows that ability is not fixed, but is a function of circumstances? As long ago as 1957, Vernon showed how the IQs of Southampton pupils in grammar schools rose by 4.9 points in four years, while those of pupils in secondary modern schools fell by 3 points. Yet the HMI paper implicitly assumes that ability is not only easily determined, but also fixed.

Adopting MAT changes the professional role of teachers. If it is done as part of a whole curriculum philosophy, it need not mean more work – simply different work. After all, the HMI secondary survey shows how little MAT has been taken up in schools, and yet how class teaching can neglect pupils at the extremes of ability: 'The stimulation that able pupils need to extend their language was lacking. . . . The less able pupils were less likely to get the teaching they need.'

What both HMI reports show is that, because there is little curriculum development in schools, MAT is usually badly done. But this is not enough to justify the apparent prejudice of HMI against it. Rather should it be an argument for showing how MAT can work, if it is undertaken as part of curriculum thinking. In moral terms, the evidence that ability is hard to measure, has no obvious relationship with attainment, and changes in different learning situations, is so overwhelming that to adopt a common curriculum without adopting MAT is a contradiction in terms. There is also the practical argument that only a mixed ability format can give all pupils easy access – under teacher direction – to the richness of resources which the common curriculum will engender. I prefer to talk of a 'mixed ability format' since it makes clear that no doctrinaire view of MAT is prescribed, and least of all that it should mean that pupils of different ability should sit side by side doing the same thing.[29] The essence is flexibility: there will be times when a form group – even perhaps a year group – will watch a demonstration or film and get quite different experiences from a common event. There will be other times when a teacher will informally arrange a small group of pupils of similar interest and capability around tables to discuss, or write a play, or work through the same questions. What will inform such judgments will be the teacher's resolution of curriculum problems, informed by the school's shared understandings and his own intuitive response.

5   Pastoral care and personal and social development

A besetting difficulty in curriculum planning is the risk that the part will come to dominate the whole. Because we build up our understanding of the curriculum from a study of its parts – of the scope of subjects, of resource-based learning, and so on – it is easy to lose sight of the whole and expect too much of some particular aspect. The tendency in the early 1970s, for example, to suppose that varied and abundant resources for learning would solve all problems has already been mentioned. The same high expectations have been entertained of mixed ability teaching. While these are both necessary attributes of a good whole curriculum, they are not alone sufficient: they cannot replace adequate planning of the curriculum. The recent emphasis on skill-based learning makes the same error. Graded criterion-referenced tests have value in a skill-based approach to the teaching of a foreign language, but have no general applicability to the whole curriculum. They are simply one element in an entire discourse of ideas.

From the mid-1960s to the mid-1970s, a distorting element of this kind was the emphasis on pastoral care. It stemmed from the view that the social development of pupils could – and should – be divorced from educational and curriculum concerns and pursued for its own sake. The distortion gained strength from the tendency for reorganised comprehensive schools to allocate academic posts to the former grammar school staff, and so-called pastoral posts (head of house, head of lower school) to staff coming from senior positions in modern schools. The effect was to drive a wedge between the 'academic' and the 'pastoral', to divide the staff of schools, and to promote a wholly mistaken view of curriculum action.

A contributing error arose from the work of some social scientists and behavioural psychologists, who chose to distinguish between 'cognitive' and 'affective' experience. Whatever convenience this might have for academic classifications, it is clear that education is to do with the development of mind, and that all our actions are the result of mind: how we get on with each other, what we think of our neighbours, the causes we sympathise with – all depend on how we think, on how we can handle the forms of knowledge and understanding which make up our culture. The business of schools is to promote these learnings, which will include learning about ourselves and our relations with others. The separation between the cognitive and affective – or, for that matter, between the academic and the pastoral – is therefore entirely bogus and, indeed, meretricious: for it presents a false view of what education and teaching are about.

There is now growing unease about the readiness with which pastoral care has been embraced by schools as an activity in its own right, and the HMI secondary survey makes no bones about the need to make the curriculum the central issue: 'Schools place great emphasis on fostering their pupils' development by means of pastoral structures and organisations. Much would be gained if equal emphasis was placed on the learning in the classroom and the teaching of an appropriate curriculum.' It is, therefore, unfortunate that the HMI fall into the self-same trap, and choose as one of the four areas studied 'personal and social development'. Since the other three are science, mathematics, and language, it is clear that PSM is to be given the status and separation of a subject in its own right. The signs are that what pastoral care was to the 1960s and 1970s, PSM will be to the 1980s.

For the same mistake is being repeated: the curriculum is being atomised, the part is being treated as the whole, and teachers will see PSM as something separate from their specialist subject work.

In schools with strong pastoral care structures, there is a tendency for staff to shrug off pupils' personal concerns as something others are paid to attend to. An emphasis on PSM in its own right will mean that subject teaching is seen as the real 'academic' work of the school, and PSM seen as something relegated to form periods or separate 'design for living' courses. The result will be precisely the reverse of what is intended: instead of enriching classroom experience, the academic will be divorced from the pastoral, and the grammar school curriculum will obtain a fresh lease of life.

The effect of all this will be to deskill teachers, by undermining their central role as educators. For a lesson on history, or metalwork, or chemistry is not merely to do with memorising this or that fact, but with establishing concepts and beliefs. Personal, social and moral development is not something confined to the DFL course on Wednesday afternoons, but an inseparable aspect of everything a teacher does. When a third year group watches the film 'Lord of the Flies' in an English or expressive arts period, they are certainly 'doing English', but they are also reflecting upon human conduct, and the teacher will make this an intrinsic part of his treatment. When a mathematics teacher discusses with a pupil his difficulties with matrix multiplication, the way he talks, the assumptions he makes about his relation with the pupil, his understanding of his previous work and its failures and successes – all these enter into teaching, and involve the teacher inescapably in the growth of the pupil's social and moral understanding. The same will be true of school organisations: the way the school connects its curriculum with assumptions about pupil grouping, about learning strategies, about resources and interrelations between subjects – these are all a reflection of an educational ideal or theory. They are the currency in which curriculum beliefs are negotiated, and these beliefs make assumptions about moral, social and personal development.

The faulty assumption is that the work of schooling can be broken down into components, much as the division of labour is celebrated in the assembly-line system of motor car manufacture. But a Swedish car manufacturer has introduced a quite different system: cars are built by teams of workers, who function as a social unit and expect each to carry out not just one task, but all the tasks needed. The result is said to be greater commitment and higher quality. Teaching, and solving curriculum problems, works better on the Volvo principle. The more readily staff can come to share problems and experiences, and use their specialism as a way of interpreting other curriculum experience, the more they will reflect upon and intellectualise about education. We need to identify the component tasks and areas of interest, but only as aspects of the whole – never as ends in themselves.

For this reason, I am uneasy about the tendency to set up a separate faculty of social education rather than make activities in health, political, careers and social education a matter for faculties directly connected with conventional areas of knowledge and experience. Simplicity is a great asset in curriculum planning: far better to make a variety of approaches and activities an intrinsic part of broad faculty areas, than establish more extrinsic divisions between subjects and faculties. I have similar reservations about attempts to establish a 'pastoral curriculum', and introduce, into form tutor periods, sessions in 'life skills' and counselling therapies. In schools offering a traditional curriculum and formal teaching to match, these approaches will certainly stimulate discussion in form periods. But the approach will be at odds with the main thrust of the curriculum, and make it easier to avoid changing it. It can be argued that 'life skills' are taken care of elsewhere.

A further danger lies in the nature of these materials, which owe much to behaviourist psychology and what has been termed in the USA the 'human potential' movement. They raise questions about the moral basis of such devices which might be subject to much greater scrutiny were they part of the normal taught curriculum. Moral and social education are important aspects of the whole curriculum which should be explicit aspects of school policy. There is a tendency for 'life skills' materials to infiltrate the curriculum via form periods without any adequate discussion of the issues involved. To decontextualise personal relationships in this way seems hardly educational.

The contentious nature of this territory stems from increasing reservations about the growth of psychotherapy.[30] Much of it is based on the 'encounter group' ideas of Carl Rogers, and assumes the truth of such propositions as that, before knowing others, you must first know yourself. Many would argue that we can only come to know ourselves through others. The danger is that by fostering self-probing devices of this kind, pupils will become introspective and withdrawn. We know so little about the effects of this approach that it would at least be wise to counsel caution. The American experience of these psychotherapy-based techniques with adults is disturbing. Schools should be wary of initiating experiments of this nature with children.

6   *Integrated studies*

Whole curriculum planning implies a fresh look at the role of subjects. The traditional curriculum is made up of a collection of separate subjects, each with its own aims and outcomes. The underlying assumption is that the aggregate of all these separate intentions will coincide with the broad aims of the school itself. This seems very difficult to justify.

But if we are to bring greater coherence to the curriculum, we must consider whether cognate subjects might be brought together so as to serve a more clearly defined common purpose. Such 'curriculum areas' might include:

1   *the humanities*: some linkage between history and geography, possibly with religious education and English as well;
2   *the sciences*: some pattern of interrelation between physics, chemistry and biology, possibly running across the years 11–16;
3   *the techno-aesthetic area*: some definition of common ground between arts and crafts, possibly including housecraft;
4   *the expressive*: some form of shared experience between music and drama, possibly linked with English or art.

There are hints of the possibility – indeed, the desirability – of most of these linkages in the discussion by HMI of Example B in *A View of the Curriculum*. But no attempt is made to pursue the issues involved, beyond mentioning the need for 'specialist teachers to rethink the definition and content of traditional subjects'.

Given the importance of subject integration, it is remarkable that so little is available in print to guide the teachers in enterprising schools preparing to tackle the task. Yet there are a number of schools – as Chapter 3 bears witness – where subject integration has been successfully undertaken. And there are a number of Schools Council projects which have fostered it. This is a void which the Council would be well placed to fill, if it were sensitive and responsive to the concerns of schools.

All I can do here is suggest that it is helpful to decide whether one is adopting a strong or a weak thesis of integration. A *strong thesis* implies that there are overarching concepts which subjugate the contributions of the components. Thus a strong thesis of integrated science would advance concepts like the transfer of energy, and devise a course which showed how such a concept could be interpreted in the three contributory disciplines. SCISP uses this approach, and this particular example is taken from the course.

A *weak thesis* of integrated science would argue that such concepts, if they exist, are less important than the structures of the separate subjects. The task of integration is then more a matter of interrelation: of cutting out dead wood in the subjects so as to expose the key elements, and looking for profitable forms of linkage which can be exploited.

In practice, of course, a number of positions may be adopted between these two extremes. The importance of epistemological inquiry, like that of Hirst and other philosophers, is that it helps us to see which style of integration is appropriate. In the case of science, it might reasonably be argued that to think scientifically – to be brought inside the nature of scientific inquiry – is an activity which transcends the separate subjects. This would then argue for a strong thesis, since none of the separate subjects could alone serve to introduce the pupil to the meaning of science. It might, of course, be argued that physics can be taught through, say, botany; but to do it would certainly involve the extension of the subject into physics, and involve the teacher in inquiries which would lie outside his normal competence. Hence the need to tackle these questions and devise a form of organisation which suits them.

In the case of humanities as an integrated area, we have to consider whether overarching concepts exist which correspond to humanities as a unique form of inquiry in its own right. Some of the schools studied in Chapter 3 adopt this strong thesis, often identifying humanities with the notion of *inquiry* (e.g. Priory School in years 1–3). Some schools have used a similar approach in years 4 and 5 with courses in social studies or humanities, using *issues* as the integrating theme.

Others would argue that humanities is not the same as science. A strong thesis is appropriate for science, where unifying concepts exist, because the methods of science – the unique property of science as a form of knowledge and understanding – are more important in a general education programme than the content areas of the separate subjects. But humanities, on the other hand, consists of separate subjects which certainly benefit from being tackled by a team of teachers looking for interlinking themes, but which would lose their identity – and therefore their educational value – if they were yoked beneath some overriding principle of procedure. This would be a weak thesis of humanities integration, and would mean that the programme was arranged so that while the course is planned on a co-operative basis and indeed often organised on the ground by means of integrating material where this seems appropriate, it will be taught by staff who are functioning as specialists and anxious to ensure that what they see as the conceptual structure and organising language of their subject is made clear to the pupil. The Sheredes School scheme for an 11–16 humanities course in Chapter 3 is of this type.

6 How common can the curriculum be?

The case studies presented in Chapter 3 show that the common curriculum can be organised so as to offer core experiences to all a school's pupils. There is, however, a tendency to argue in some quarters that there are pupils whose interests would not be well served by a common curriculum. It is suggested that pupils in this 'grey area' need some singular provision of their own.

In the main, I think this position arises from a misunderstanding of how a common curriculum works in practical terms. It is not a uniform curriculum; it does not seek to offer identical experiences to pupils of different interests and capacities and backgrounds. Rather, it determines key forms of cultural experience – knowledge and understanding of various aspects of our society – and then seeks to bring pupils inside these experiences by a variety of methods.[31] There is no evidence to show that schools cannot make a common curriculum work in these terms: on the contrary, the evidence of schools like those cited in Chapter 3 is that such a curriculum reveals unsuspected talents in all pupils.

The 'grey area', in short, appears to be a figment of the imagination: an invented category of pupils which does not correspond to any identifiable property of the pupils thus labelled. If a school has had to identify a 'grey area', it is a sign of a defective curriculum, not of defective pupils. Most commonly it is the result of allowing a subject-centred, recall-dominated grammar-school curriculum to influence the whole programme of the school. If the emphasis in years 4 and 5 is on examination success first and education second, there will be a group of pupils who fail to fit in with the assumptions of this model. Some of them may be of 'academic' ability: they have always existed in the lower streams of grammar schools. Others will have divergent minds and want to see how knowledge can be used, rather than stored. They will vote with their feet, and in extreme cases will be hived off into separate option bands or teaching groups, much as 'Newsom children' were in the late 1960s. There is nothing ineducable about them, just as there is nothing constitutionally defective about sufferers from rickets. They, too, have a deficiency disease; they suffer from a deficient curriculum – as, indeed, do their peers in the academic option groups. But the limitations of an academic diet are masked by short-term success.

Talk of the 'grey area', of 'underachieving pupils' is also a self-fulfilling prophecy. If we have low expectations of pupils, they will please us by conforming to them. The success of schools operating a common curriculum shows that categories like 'Newsom children' do violence to the capability and innate responsiveness of all children. The same is true of academic attempts, like that of Bantock,[32] to argue that while academic pupils need a grammar-school style of curriculum, for the less able a 'folk' curriculum is all that is appropriate. Pleas of this kind for a latter-day bipartite curriculum are as unconvincing now as they were in the 1940s and 1950s. Not only do they deny the common humanity of people; they miss the point that the task of mass education is to devise an appropriate, common but non-uniform curriculum for all.

A powerful influence on this kind of thinking is the growing enthusiasm for post-16 courses based on what might be termed the manpower view of training. Fashionable rhetoric suggests that too much can be made of the distinction between education and training, and that – at least for some pupils – a 14–16 curriculum based on 'experiential learning' and 'social and life skills' is called for. It is then an easy step to argue that the 14–18 curriculum should be seen as a continuum, with a strong emphasis on what is industrially relevant.[33]

I think this line of reasoning should be resisted. To educate is to transform a student's view of the world: to train is to inculcate a skill worth nothing beyond itself. It is, of course, possible to devise a vocational programme which is treated in an educative way: but this is to say nothing more than that, in education, *how* you do it is as important as *what* you do. And giving a programme a vocational bias – however slight – constrains the range of experiences which can be offered. Post-16, there is much to be said for sustaining broad educational courses at a variety of levels which are built, to some extent, around a focus of student interest which may well be vocational. But this can be justified only because, pre-16, the student has been offered a common curriculum which equips him for personal autonomy and cultural judgment.

To divide 14–16 pupils into different categories for different kinds of curricula seems to me quite indefensible, if the task of secondary schooling is to offer all a liberal education. And no other form of education will equip our pupils for the kinds of decision making and problem solving they will need to make in the post-industrial adult world of political instability and advanced technology. To label certain pupils as vocational rather than academic is to commit a sizeable proportion of the population to stigmatised schooling: nothing less than an act of political castration. Post-16 developments must not divert us from the need to offer all pupils a common 11–16 curriculum.

Exercise 5: simulation study: Brobdingnag School

General

Brobdingnag School was reorganised as a comprehensive from a former grammar school seven years ago. It saw rapid growth in its early years, but recently rolls have fluctuated around 7 fe and will fall sharply in the future.

Pupils leave at 16 and both an FE and sixth form college are available. The school serves a country town with an overspill housing estate and a private estate popular with commuters. The surrounding area, from which other pupils come, is largely rural. Some parents choose to send their children to 11–18 comprehensives or independent schools in a town some seven miles away.

Staffing data

Swiftshire staffs its 11–16 schools as follows:

Year 1	23:1	Year 4	17:1
Year 2	23:1	Year 5	16.5:1
Year 3	22:1		

At present there are 1109 pupils on roll, as follows:

Year 1	205	Year 4	213
Year 2	229	Year 5	249
Year 3	213		

The curriculum structure of the school at present is given in Figure 2.1 on pages 105 and 106. In all, this curriculum requires 1931 teacher periods (tps). They are distributed as follows (this may be verified from the data given in the diagram):

103

Year 1	314	Year 4	428
Year 2	370	Year 5	473
Year 3	346		

The total staffing available, by application of the county ratios, is 56.17. Thus the contact ratio for staff is

$$\frac{1931}{40 \times 56.17} = 0.86.$$

Falling rolls

The authority predicts that first year numbers will be as follows:

1981	178	1984	144	1987	126
1982	196	1985	120		
1983	145	1986	130		

These figures have been discussed with the school, and it has been agreed that the staff loss in each year shall be as follows:

1981	−2.0	1984	−4.5	1987	−4.0
1982	−0.5	1985	−4.0		
1983	−3.0	1986	−2.5		

Simulation issues

Assume the present head retired at the end of the previous term, in December. You have been presented with these data on taking office in the following January.

The school is competently run, and you have two able deputies. But staff morale is depressed, and the school has a lack-lustre feel. You sense, from your appointment interviews and subsequent conversation with the chairman of governors, that you have a mandate to 'shake things up a bit'. The chief education officer mentioned your previous experience as deputy head in a school operating a common curriculum, and added: 'With all this Circular 6/81 business, I hope you'll give us a bit of a lead and shows us all what we ought to do.' In particular, you recognise that as the school falls from 7 to 4 forms of entry by 1985, some new curriculum thinking will be needed. The staff are also concerned at growing youth unemployment in the area.

Form No. Periods per subject per week (total 40)

Form	No.				Ga					
1P	30	M_6 E_6 G_2 H_2			Ga	S_4	F_4	Wk Hk_2	Mk Nk_2	A_2 Re_2 Mu_2 Pe_2 Dr_2
1W	31	" " " "			Ga	"	"	"	"	" " " " "
1R	31	" " " "			Ga	"	"	"	"	" " " " "
1E	30	" " " "			Ga	"	"	"	"	" " " " "
1S	28	M_8 Is_{12}			Ga	S_2 Rs_4		Wk		A_2 Re_2 Mu_2 Pe Dr_2
1C	28	" "			Ga	" "		Mk		" " " Pe "
1H	27	" "			Ga	" "		Hk		" " " Pe "
		+ Rm ⌐⎯⎯⎯ 16			Ga_2			Nk_4		Pe_2
2P	30	M E_5 G_2 H_2			Ga	S_4	F	Wk Hk_2	Mk Nk_2	A_2 Re_2 Mu_2 Pe_2 L
2W	30	M " " "			Ga	"	F	"	"	" " " " L
2R	29	M " " "			Ga	"	F	"	"	" " " " Gm
2E	31	M_5 " " "			Ga	"	F_4	"	"	" " " " Gm_4
2S	27	M E Is_6			Ga	S_2 Rs_4		Wk		A_2 Mu_2 Pe Dr_2
2C	27	M E "			Ga	" "		Mk		" " Pe "
2H	28	M E "			Ga	" "		Hk		" " Pe "
2N	27	M E "			Ga	" "		Nk		" " Pe "
		6⎯8 + Rm ⌐⎯⎯ 28			Ga_2			Td_4		Pe_2
3P	32	M E G_2 H_2			Ga	B C P	F	Wk		A_2 Re_2 Pe_2 L
3W	30	M E " "			Ga	B C P	F	Mk Nk		" " " L
3R	32	M E " "			Ga	B C P	F	2Hk Td		" " " Gm
3E	32	M_5 E_5 " "			Ga	B_2 C_2 P_2	F_4	Ct_4		" " " Gm_4
3S	29	M E G_3 H_3			Ga	S		Wk		A_2 Mu_2 Pe Dr_2
3C	30	M E " "			Ga	S		Mk Hk		" " Pe "
3H	28	M E " "			Ga	S		Nk		" " Pe "
		M E 6⎯8			Ga_2	S_6		Td_4		Pe_2

Figure 2.1 Brobdingnag School curriculum structure

105

Year 4

Class	No.					Options (upper band)					
4P	32	M	E	Ga	DFL	2Mk	2F Mu B H T	L Gm C G T Wk	2F 2B 2H Ec	2C 2G Re Mk A	2P Gm L Pc Hk Co
4W	32	M	E	Ga	DFL	2Wk Mv					
4R	33	M	E	Ga	DFL	2Hk					
4E	31	M (5)	E (6)	Ga	DFL	2A	(4)	(4)	(4)	(4)	(4)
				Ga	DFL	2Td					

Class	No.					Options (lower band)				
4S	28	M	E	Ga	DFL	2Nk	2P Wk T Co	2Bh Mk T Re	Td A Mv G Hk	Td A Rs H Hk
4C	29	M	E	Ga	DFL	Ct				
4H	28	M (5)	E (6)	Ga (2)	DFL (3)	Po (4)	(5)	(5)	(5)	(5)

Year 5

Class	No.					Options (upper band)					
5P	30	M	E	Ga	DFL	2Mk	2F Mu B H G Hk T	L Gm C G Hk H T Wk	2F 2B 2H Ec Mu	2C 2G Re Mk Rs	2P Gm L Pc Hk Co A
5W	29	M	E	Ga	DFL	2Wk					
5R	28	M	E	Ga	DFL	Mv					
5E	30	M	E	Ga	DFL	2Hk					
5G	29	M (6)	E (5)	Ga	DFL	2A	(4)	(4)	(4)	(4)	(4)
				Ga	DFL	2Td					

Class	No.					Options (lower band)				
5S	25	M	E	Ga	DFL	Ct	2P Wk T Co Nk	2Bh Mk T Co Re	Td 2A Mv G Hk	Td A Rs H Hk Mu
5C	27	M	E	Ga	DFL	Ph				
5H	26	M	E	Ga	DFL	2Nk				
5N	25	M (6)	E (5)	Ga (2)	DFL (3)	2Po (4)	(5)	(5)	(5)	(5)

Notes

1 *Examinations*: DFL is not examined. Mv, Ph and Mu are CSE Mode 3 courses. Otherwise, it should be assumed that subjects lead to O level GCE and to CSE in the upper band, and to CSE – or are non-examined – in the lower band.

2 All students select one art or craft subject from the core pool in years 4 and 5.

In planning your changes, you may assume that staff are not opposed to innovation and that some in-service support will be available. Staff will be prepared to change roles and the authority will facilitate transfer of scaled post points to a limited extent. LEA support will depend on the conviction with which you can present a new rationale and justify it to staff and governors.

General considerations

In responding to these issues, you may find it helpful to refer to four factors which determine curriculum decisions, which imply social and moral judgments, and which can each work at two levels: they can be seen in relation to *ephemeral* issues (falling rolls, vocationalism, microprocessors) or *perennial* problems (general education and the needs of specialists, national needs and local conditions). Your judgment of these factors constitutes – in its aggregate effect – the underpinning *rationale* of the design:

1   *Social milieux* – factors to do with world problems, national concerns and local issues, e.g. is competition more important than co-operation? What should be the place of political education in the curriculum? What meaning can we give to the notion of the community school?
2   *Pupils and learning* – how do pupils learn? What factors help the process? What conditions help children become persons?
3   *Teachers and teaching* – what resources do a school's staff offer? How can they be used most effectively? What limitations are imposed?
4   *Subject matter* – what should we teach? How should the subject matter of teaching be chosen so as to do justice to particular forms of knowledge or aspects of the culture? What should we select from our culture?

(This analysis into four time-scale dependent factors is adapted from Schwab (1963).)

The following considerations may bear upon your analysis of the present curriculum:

1   A banded structure runs for all five years. Is this justified?
2   Setting policies vary between subjects. Is this justified?
3   Integrated studies have been established in years 1–3, but only in the lower band. Should this be extended – or eliminated?
4   The curriculum varies between the bands. Is this justified?
5   Remedial work by withdrawal is confined to years 1 and 2. Should this be extended?
6   Are there subjects which appear to be given an unusual emphasis in years 1–3? Is this emphasis a function of ability bands? Are there subjects which appear to be neglected?
7   What rationale underlies the core-plus-options scheme in years 4 and 5?

8 How is the available staffing distributed over the five years? Are there points of particular richness, at the expense of other years?

9 What might appear to be areas of particular strength among the staff – where there are signs of innovation and invention?

10 What areas appear to be less ready to respond to new ideas and the forces of change?

11 What part of the curriculum is most likely to be influenced by falling rolls?

12 What parts of the curriculum should change, if the new structure is to offer all pupils a curriculum that is broad, balanced and coherent?

13 How might it be possible to make these changes and at the same time develop a curriculum which would present more innate flexibility and thus adapt more readily to the effect of falling rolls?

14 What changes might result in the school's examinations policy?

15 What areas would you single out as needing support from an in-service programme?

Lines of solution

This study may be tackled at a number of levels. Here are three suggestions: they may be adapted to meet local circumstances.

1 Most briefly, but to good effect, it is possible simply to take the present structure as displayed and discuss its weaknesses. If discussion group time is limited to two or three hours, it is pointless to attempt much more.

2 A more advanced treatment would go further and set out the general lines of a new curriculum, using the outline of the problem as presented but without any attempt to cost the new curriculum in too much detail. This has been found to work very satisfactorily with groups of six or seven teachers spending a total of about six or eight hours *in toto*. Results can be put onto an acetate sheet and discussed among groups.

3 One can go further and use the data on staff decline to see exactly what the new scheme means in terms of staff and their responsibility post points. If falling rolls were a particular emphasis, groups could go on to show how the designation of staff might be phased. This would need twelve hours or more.

Chapter 3

Case studies and school decisions: the curriculum in practice

Secondary school case studies

This chapter illustrates the process of curriculum change by examining the curriculum structures of a number of schools which have embarked on whole curriculum planning. This is a convenient way of exposing the priorities and problems of secondary schools, since the curriculum structure inevitably encapsulates a series of discussions and decisions and allows the observer to admire a neat device here, or question a puzzling element there. The structures offered are in no case seen as immutable solutions: in some cases, they are very evidently stages in a process and the capacity for change is built into them. In others, they have reached a state of stability after a period of appraisal but new developments will lead to fresh responses.

The seven schools which form the subjects of the case studies have been chosen because they each have adopted – or are in the course of adopting – a common curriculum 11–16 or 13–16, but in different circumstances. Fig. 3.1 summarises this.

Each school has chosen to take the notion of a common or core curriculum and develop it in its own context and for its own reasons. The different circumstances of the schools lead to considerable variation between the structures which result. At the same time, common problems recur and these hark back to Chapters 1 and 2 in this book. By reflecting on the different ways in which these familiar problems are tackled, the reader may gain insight into the practical tasks of curriculum planning – into the ideals and compromises which are necessary to make ideas work effectively.

After each presentation of the school's curriculum structure

SCHOOL	Has a sixth form	Serves mainly rural area	Experience of falling rolls	Started from scratch	Complete 11-16 common corriculum	Complete 13-16 common corriculum
Berkeley Vale	✓	✓			✓	
Carisbrooke	✓		✓			✓
Gillotts			✓			
Holsworthy		✓				
Kingshill		✓		✓	✓	
Priory				✓	✓	
Sheredes	✓			✓	✓	

Figure 3.1

some questions are offered which raise issues arising from the solution the school has adopted. In some cases, these are followed by comments on the questions, drawing attention to matters of particular interest. The absence of these further comments should not be taken, however, as an indication that a case study is less interesting than others; simply that the matters which arise have already been discussed in other parts of the book. It is also likely that the reader will prefer to be left to his own ruminations on at least some occasions, and not be subjected too relentlessly to my own opinions and predilections. In some cases, it has been possible to list further reading which will provide more information about a school than has been possible in these summaries.

Although I have tried very hard to present an accurate account of each school's curriculum, I must accept responsibility for any errors which may have crept in. I am particularly conscious of the compressed description I have frequently had to give of an organisational device or examination programme which deserves a great deal more space. This is certainly true of some of the Mode 3 programmes which have been developed in these schools, and which represent not only a great deal of careful thought on paper, but an enormous amount of skilled and enterprising teaching in the classroom. And in any event, a brief written account of the kind offered here can do only scant justice to the reality of the curriculum experience offered in real schools.

1   Berkeley Vale School, Berkeley, Gloucestershire

This is an 11–18 mixed 3/4 form entry comprehensive school serving a dispersed, mainly rural area around the small town of Berkeley, near Bristol. Over half the pupils travel to the school by school bus. It is remote from competing secondary schools and therefore has a full-range comprehensive intake.

Berkeley Vale School was reorganised as a comprehensive (from a secondary modern school) in 1971. Until 1975, the school operated along conventional lines, with 35 periods of 40 minutes per week and a conventional option scheme in years 4 and 5. The problems of accommodating a variety of subjects within this format in a small school gave extra impetus to a process of rethinking the curriculum which had begun in 1973, when the head (David Payne) encouraged staff to reflect upon educational issues by delegating decisions and posing questions. Thus the team of first year tutors found themselves considering the question: what should the pupils be learning, and how should the learning be organised?

The head's main aim was to 'put the staff in a mood for change. . . . It would take time.' The current of change shaped up around the discussions on the pastoral side – of the year and form tutors. 'A teacher might say quite different things, as a head of department or as a tutor.' By 1975, these discussions had led to the wider adoption of mixed ability teaching, and the identification of the third year as an unsatisfactory bridge between a broad curriculum and the options of the fourth year. At this stage, too, groups began to consider theoretical approaches to the curriculum, in particular those of Hirst and Phenix. Again, the pastoral teams were the active agents in producing lists of forms and fields of knowledge.

Attempts to approach the core curriculum by asking specialist staff to pronounce on, say, the needs of society or of the child in relation to this or that subject, were unfruitful. But asking them how a faculty might be linked with their subject was rewarding. Faculty groups began to form, and as staff increasingly identified with these broader forms of organisation so the design of a common curriculum took shape. The climate of change had become established. The original concern with pupils as persons was sustained: the intention to run regular camps for each year 'so as to get to know the children better' emerged at this time.

In 1976, the school was ready to implement a radically new curriculum organised into eight faculties and using block timetabling. The existing fifth year would have to continue with the old core-plus-options timetable. The new scheme could be introduced piecemeal, a year at a time; or *en bloc* to years 1–4, at the cost of some considerable inconvenience to staff in making the new system fit. The staff decided to accept some unreasonable personal timetables for the sake of installing the new curriculum as soon as possible. From September 1976 years 1–4 adopted a 10-day timetable based on four 75-minutes periods each day. A year later, the system had been extended to all five years, and the sixth form, too, had been incorporated within the system, using as basis the same block timetable on a two-day module. (See section on Timetabling below.) The emphasis was on implementing the new structure: 'We knew the administrative problems could be overcome. Our aim was to get the curriculum right first, and tidy up afterwards.'

In summer 1981 the first group of pupils to experience the new curriculum exclusively took 16-plus examinations: the results exceeded the hopes of staff and confirmed feelings that the common curriculum had enhanced pupil expectations: 'Our new curriculum changed attitudes. Children can do much more than you think they can do. And every child matters.' Of the 81 children in this fifth year group, 22 obtained 5 or more ABC O level grades or grade 1 CSE; 62 at least one pass at these grades. Only two pupils were ungraded in science, where a common curriculum had been followed for five years.

Because of its remoteness, the school must also offer a sixth form. Staffing cuts have made it difficult to sustain some curriculum refinements 11–18, but fourteen subjects are offered to A level in the sixth form and from September 1981, the 11–16 curriculum was modified – as a result of further staff discussions – so as to include a single period of social education for all pupils. Notes 1 and 9 on the curriculum structure diagram (Figure 3.2) indicate how this was done, and the number of weekly periods thus increased from 20 to 21.

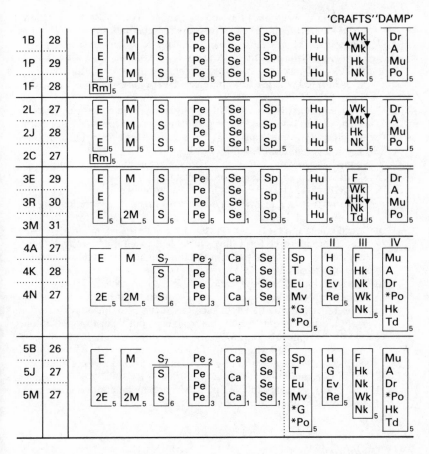

Figure 3.2 Berkeley Vale School curriculum structure

Notes

* Subjects likely to be withdrawn from the option scheme due to cuts.

** Drama, Art, Music, Pottery.

1 There are four periods of 1 1/4 hours daily, except on Thursdays, when there are five periods of 1 hour. Four of these Thursday periods conform to the normal pattern; the fifth is blocked across the entire school as Se.

2 English is treated as 'Communications Study' and examined at Mode 3 O level (AEB: 50 per cent marks for course work) and CSE (60 per cent course work).

113

3 Mathematics is a school-devised course based on SMP and using some RLDU material and 'Oxford Resource Mathematics'.
4 Humanities integrates Re, H and G using five main topics – Exploration Man; Survival; Ancient Civilisations; The Vale of Berkeley; Britain and the World. From the third year subjects are differentiated with greater emphasis. History uses Schools Council History 13–16 Project.
5 Science in years 1–3 is a school-devised integrated course. In years 4 and 5, all pupils take a double-subject integrated course. Abler pupils take SCISP (note increased time allocation at expense of Pe). The rest take equivalent double-subject CSE.
6 Spanish follows the Schools Council *Adelante* course throughout.
7 'Crafts' uses a 10-week module for rotation.
8 'DAMP' (Dp) offers one lesson to each pupil in each contributory subject per fortnight, with a good deal of integrated work leading to year plays and productions.
9 Social education (see note 1) is taught in year teams, made up of the year tutor and three form tutors in each year. Of the hour available, half is used as material preparation time for staff while pupils end school 30 minutes early.
10 The four options in years 4 and 5 are listed here as I, II, III and IV, but in the school are known as languages, humanities, crafts and arts: they essentially continue the eight-faculty structure established in years 1–3. One subject must be chosen from each option group, and at least two subjects must be either a foreign language, a craft or one of the expressive arts 'DAMP' group. Pupils may thus take two humanities subjects or two craft subjects. Pupils taking Sp and F would take one Hu subject and Hk or Td from DAMP.
11 Half periods are possible in Sp, E, M and S by timetabling these against each other (see note on timetabling).

Summary

The Berkeley Vale curriculum offers all pupils common curriculum experiences with remarkably little differentiation by ability in its formal structure. It uses integrated studies and team teaching to good effect. Adopting a simple structure of eight faculties (which are converted to options in years 4 and 5), each with the same time allocation, makes for a particularly simple solution to the timetabling problem. The introduction of social education after five years shows that, even so, the scheme is flexible and can respond to changed circumstances. The school makes good use of available project materials (e.g. SCISP, Schools Council History 13–16) and the block timetabling allows considerable flexibility in staffing. This is particularly important in a small school. The thorough-going common curriculum has evolved from a traditional curriculum in an established school, with little help from outside agencies. The following extract from a staff document of 1976 illustrates the extent to which the curriculum was seen as the central concern, along with a concept of education itself:

The curriculum must take account of:

1 individual children;
2 society;
3 modes of knowledge and understanding;
4 distinctive yet generalised human abilities in the domains of thinking, feeling and acting.

The six main stages in our plan are:

1 consideration of the curriculum including a decision as to whether it should be divided or common;
2 decision on the broad areas of the curriculum;
3 fitting or not of existing subjects into the broad areas of (2);
4 production of pattern of likely subject or 'faculty' areas and staff teams;
5 consultation with careers advisers to avoid unreal solutions being preferred, and feedback of this information to staff;
6 construction of a basic timetable module for approval by the staff.

Timetabling

The Berkeley Vale timetable adopts the 'consistent blocking' system. This works best when the separate timetable elements are of nearly equal size. In this case all eight elements of the basic timetable (social education being a 'stop the clock' addition – see note 1 above) are of exactly equal size. Since each is allocated five periods, the basic timetable must have a span of forty periods or two weeks. However, the core of this 10-day timetable need be only two days in size. The other eight days may be formed simply by repeating the eight modules which make up the two-day core (see Table 3.1).

TABLE 3.1

Year	Monday				Tuesday			
1	Hu	Sp/M	S	Dp	Cr	M/Sp	Pe	E
2	Pe	M/Sp	Cr	S	Dp	Sp/M	E	Hu
3	S/Dp	Hu	Dp/E	M/Sp	Sp/M	E/S	Cr	Pe
4	M	Pe	Hu	Cr	E	Dp	S	Sp
5	Cr	Dp	M	E	S/Pe	Hu	Sp	S
Modules	a	b	c	d	e	f	g	h

The modules a–h are now the building blocks of the entire timetable. Thus Wednesday's timetable may be written: b a d c. In order to give each faculty its requisite five periods over the two weeks, it is only necessary to vary the timetable for one day in the second week. This largely eliminates the confusion caused for pupils and staff when a 10-day timetable means two completely different weeks.

The complete school timetable for years 1–5 may now be written:

MON	TUES	WED	THURS 1	THURS 2	FRI
abcd	efgh	badc	cd*hb	eg*fa	gfha

* is social education.

Note that in Table 3.1:
  (i) Sp/M in years 1 and 2 indicates half periods;
  (ii) S/Dp in year 3 indicates that 2 groups have S while the other 2 groups have Dp, and so on;
  (iii) In year 5, S/Pe is in fact arranged as $S_2/Pe_7/Ca_1$ over two weeks. This indicates the flexibility of block timetabling.

Exercise 6: Berkeley Vale School

1 Although the intake is full range comprehensive, remedial provision is confined to English extraction. Is this enough?
2 What are likely to be the components of the Se course? Could they be incorporated within the eight faculties?
3 Only mathematics is setted in years 1–3 (and only in the third year). Is more differentiation by ability desirable?
4 Spanish is an unusual choice for the first foreign language. How might it be justified?
5 French, the second foreign language, is introduced in year 3 as an option against the 'Crafts' group of subjects. Should this

116

be a free option? Is this a satisfactory solution to the second language problem? What alternatives come to mind?

6   Looking at the 11–16 curriculum, does it have the structure of a continuum? Or does there appear to be a break in the rhythm between years 1–3 and years 4,5? In what sense might year 3 be regarded as a transitional year?

7   In years 4 and 5, what proportion of the total time is basic core? To what extent do the composition of the four options, and the constraints upon choice within them, effectively extend the common core?

8   Is the single period of careers an effective provision? How else might it be offered?

9   English is separate from the humanities faculty over all five years. Is this desirable?

10   To what extent is balance across the curriculum retained in years 4 and 5? Is the provision for science too large?

11   In years 1–3, is the time allocation for physical education too large?

12   This curriculum has evolved in a school free from direct competition with neighbouring schools. Is this likely to be a factor favouring innovation?

Comments on questions

1   The absence of a separate remedial form suggests that the staff have successfully extended the concept of the common curriculum to all pupils – not only in terms of expectation, but in terms of a supple range of learning strategies incorporated within normal faculty provision.

2   Evidently the Se course covers work in health education, and also social and moral topics which might have found their way into Re provision. Whereas Re is a part of Hu in years 1–3, it is not a core element in years 4 and 5. So far, the staff have liked the Se course and think it is helping to establish better relationships with pupils, although its resource demands in terms of reprographic material are considerable. It may be relevant that the new curriculum structure originated from discussions among pastoral teams, and a 1976 document records that one tutor team 'were worried that the curriculum was the only thing being considered, it was not necessarily the most important thing in organising a school and not necessarily the most important thing at the beginning of a child's school career'. The key point is how broadly one defines the

curriculum. It may be that the recent introduction into the curriculum of social education as a separate element harks back to earlier uncertainties about the cognitive and the affective. One wonders whether the health education component of Se might not be incorporated within Pe, and the other aspects of Re and Me within Hu by extending it into a five-year core component.

3   All too often mathematics setting begins in the first year. And the third year device of one top set and two lower parallel sets seems a sensible compromise. Note that English is not setted until years 4 and 5, where it forms one top set, two parallel sets and some remedial extraction.

4   Spanish is held by some modern linguists to be more readily accessible in the early years to children of all abilities. But there is some prejudice against it on the part of parents and governing bodies.

5   French is not a free option: it is offered only to pupils with some linguistic ability as shown by their work for two years in Spanish, along with year tutors' recommendations. The usual set size is about fifteen. The option against craft is – as discussed in Chapter 2 – a common but rather unsatisfactory solution to a difficult problem, especially for a small school.

6   The only perturbation in the third year comes from setting in mathematics and the introduction of a French set by ability. But the four-option system in years 4 and 5 breaks the common broad-core 11–16 curriculum, and the school itself tends to think in terms of years 1 and 2 as identical; of year 3 as marking a transition to a different pattern in years 4 and 5.

7   The basic core takes up 55 per cent of the time. The constraints on option choice mean that an expressive or creative art is almost certain to be chosen, but there is no requirement to choose history or geography in Hu after year 3, although this option emerges – in operational terms – from Hu in years 1–3. A pupil might choose T, Re, Hk and A from the four options. The curriculum for years 4 and 5 is an improvement on Munn, in that all pupils do integrated, rather than separate subject, science; but both the social sciences and the aesthetic domain are – as with Munn – a subject choice which may not guarantee much breadth. On the other hand, the scheme makes it possible for a pupil to take SCISP and two foreign languages, while still taking a humanities subject and a creative subject from blocks II and IV. This is a considerable achievement for a small school. It could be argued that the price paid for this is a curriculum biased rather towards mathematics, science and craft at the expense of the humanities. Sustaining Hu as a core element

for five years, with enough time to lead to a double subject examination output, would correct this. But the school has considered this and found that staffing constraints would be considerable. As it stands, one could categorise this fourth and fifth year curriculum as 'improved Munn': science has been properly incorporated into the core (although all must take it as a double subject), and the 4-option system in effect reduces to Munn's two remaining core fields, social studies and creative arts, with access to two foreign languages corresponding to the Munn elective area.

8   Isolated single periods may easily be ineffective. How far provision for careers lectures, talks, visits, etc. needs to be timetabled – rather than offered *ad hoc* as needed – is debatable. Could careers education be seen as an aspect of social education, and linked with it? Shotgun marriages of this kind tidy up the timetable but only work well if they reflect staff interest. The single period might be the safer choice.

9   My own preference is for English as part of a humanities faculty. But then this faculty becomes much larger, making consistent blocking of the timetable more difficult and also requiring considerable powers of faculty leadership. There is no right answer: but it seems desirable that where English is a separate entity, it fosters good links with humanities as a cognate area of inquiry.

10   Note 7 above deals with curriculum breadth and touches on the question of balance. The case for requiring all pupils to take double science at O level (SCISP, in this case) or CSE seems to me a weak one: a single or double integrated science choice is preferable. But the advantage of the total solution is that it simplifies organisation considerably, and firmly puts paid to the idea of single subject sciences running alongside integrated courses. It is perhaps worth remarking that in this curriculum, core Hu in years 1–3 and the Hu option in years 4 and 5 are thought to have a reinforcing influence on the core science programme, which stresses the social and humanitarian issues associated with science.

11   Certainly the Pe provision is well above the norm, which would be nearer to two than five periods weekly (of 75 minutes). If five periods were necessary to ensure parity with other faculties, a broader range of activities (perhaps including health or movement and dance education) could be attempted. The equivalent weightings of the eight faculties simplify timetabling, but are they essential to the concept of balance?

12   My own view is that parental choice tends to reinforce the

status quo and inhibit change, except in the rare case of the public mood favouring educational innovation (as seemed to happen with primary education during the mid-1960s). However, the curriculum at Berkeley Vale was the subject of discussion with parents and governors before its adoption. Even so, the absence of a competing school retaining a traditional curriculum was probably a helpful influence. It should be added that in the case of innovations like SCISP, the school took pains to explain the course and the qualifications it led to to both parents and employers, and as a result has not found employers in the Bristol area to be averse to SCISP. Although Berkeley Vale School was spared the excesses of local competition, great care was taken to ensure that the new curriculum was acceptable to the school's constituency.

2   Carisbrooke School, Isle of Wight

This is a 13–18 mixed 12 form entry comprehensive school serving a mixed urban and rural area and fed by four middle schools. Since 1974 it has operated a common curriculum 13–16 followed by a sixth form on traditional lines. The school has found its curriculum successful with staff, pupils and parents, and in 1980 it was chosen by HMI as an example of a UK comprehensive for a Council of Europe visit. In addition, the number of pupils on roll has fallen from 1500 to 1100 over the period 1976–80; the (delayed) building of a new 13–18 school brought overcrowding to an end through reducing the yearly intake by about 100 pupils. The curriculum had to be resilient enough to cope with this decline, and has been the subject of a separate study (Briault and Smith, 1980). Despite fewer teachers, the common curriculum has made it possible to sustain a wide range of activities for all pupils.

The educational arguments underpinning this curriculum are evident from a paper prepared by the head (Peter Cornall) in 1979:

> Our curriculum starts from what we have come to see as the needs of the *whole person*, not just the examination candidate and not just the future worker. It therefore includes subjects and themes . . . because they contribute to that education of the whole person. Considerations of examination success and of vocational preparation are of course important to us, but they cannot have an absolute priority. . . . This is why we cannot allow the courses being followed by different groups of students

to diverge so far that their choice of future opportunities has been restricted years before the stage of even partial self-understanding has been reached.

The implementation of a common curriculum is the more remarkable in a 13–18 school, since the variety of courses in the different contributory schools means that before the secondary school can begin its programme pupils may already have taken divergent paths. During a visit to Carisbrooke, I was told that 'most of the staff here would be happy to get the pupils when they are younger'. This effect may account for the evidence in the HMI secondary survey that, at least in respect of the personal development of pupils, '13 to 18 comprehensive schools were markedly less successful than 11 or 12 to 18 full range comprehensive schools'. But Carisbrooke has overcome these difficulties and devised a structure which guarantees a broad and balanced curriculum for every pupil. This is displayed in Figure 3.3. The notes should be read carefully, since this curriculum notation was developed to display the conventional, differentiated curricula of traditional schools and does not lend itself at all conveniently to the display of common curriculum schemes.

Summary

The Carisbrooke curriculum is a broad-core programme which avoids any open option pools in years 4 and 5. There are internal subject options within CA, S, languages, and Ws – four closed pools.

Two further features of the school organisation should be noted. First, 'Guidance' has been given much thought, and is built into SRS (see page 123). Year and group tutors are also part of the scheme, and pupils complete a 'student interest form' every year to encourage self-appraisal. School records are detailed (nine assessment grades for attainment, five for effort) and a leaving testimonial is available incorporating the student's 'personal record assessment' by the group tutor. Second, the school has made vigorous efforts to establish links with industry and more than half the fifth year take up places for a week's work experience.

Exercise 7: Carisbrooke School

1 Does the subject-based provision for CA provide adequate core experiences 13–16?

		CA							SRS
3A	30	Wk	M	F	E	Pe	S	Ws	Me
		Mk			E	Pe			
3B	29	Nk	M	F	E	Pe	S	Ws	Re
		Hk			E	Pe			
3C	28	A	M	F	E $_3$	Pe $_2$	S	Ws	He
		Po							
		Mu							
3D	31	Td $_2$	M $_3$	F $_2$	+ Gm (1 + 1) $_2$		S $_3$	Ws $_3$	Ca $_2$
3E	31	Wk	M	F	E	Pe	S	Ws	Me
		Mk			E	Pe			
3F	30	Nk	'M	F	E	Pe	S	Ws	Re
		Hk			E	Pe			
3G	29	A	M	F	E	Pe	S	Ws	He
		Po			E	Pe			
		Mu							
3H	29	Td $_2$	M $_3$	F $_2$	+ Gm (1 + 1) $_2$		S $_3$	Ws $_3$	Ca $_2$
3J	28	Wk	M	F	E	Pe	S	Ws	Me
		Mk			E	Pe			
3K	31	Nk	M	F	E	Pe	S	Ws	Re
		Hk			E	Pe			
3L	30	A	M	F	E $_3$	Pe $_2$	S	Ws	He
		Po							
		Mu							
3M	30	Td $_2$	M $_3$	F $_2$	+ L (1 + 1) $_2$		S $_3$	Ws $_3$	Ca $_2$

4A , 5A		CA	S					Ws	SRS
		S	Wk	F	M	E	Pe	H	2Me
4B	5B		Mk	F	M	E	Pe	H	
		S	Nk	F	M	E	Pe		
4C	5C					E	Pe	G	2Re
4D	5D	S	Hk	Gm	M	E	Pe	G	
			A	Eu	M	E	Pe		2He
4E	5E	S	Dr	**	M	E $_3$	Pe $_2$	Bi	
4F	5F	S	Mu	L $_2$	M $_2$	+ Gm, L (1 + 1) $_2$		Bi $_4$	2Ca $_1$
4G	5G	2Wk	S	F	M	E	Pe	H	2Me
		2Mk	S	F	M	E	Pe	H	
4H	5H	Nk	S	F	M	E	Pe		
		Hk	S			E		G	2Re
4J	5J	A	S	Gm	M	E	Pe	G	
4K	5K	Td	S	Eu	M	E	Pe		2He
		Dr	S			E			
4L	5L	Mu	S	**	M	E $_3$	Pe $_2$	Bi	
		Mv	S					Bi	
4M	5M	(*) $_4$	S $_2$	L $_2$	M $_2$	+ Gm, L (1 + 1) $_2$		Bi $_4$	2Ca $_1$

Figure 3.3 Carisbrooke School curriculum structure

Notes
  *One link course available at FE college (from a choice of courses).
  **See note 10 to this figure.

1 There are four periods of 70 minutes daily. An identical timetable is offered to the three third year populations, except for variations in the choice of a second foreign language (see note 3). The two fourth year populations have an identical programme. The structure of the fifth year is identical with that of the fourth.

2 For the first half term in the third year, pupils are taught in tutor groups. Thereafter F,M are arranged in attainment sets, while E and Ws form small sets for slow learners.

3 A second foreign language is provided from entry for those choosing either Gm or L. Allocation to third year population depends on this choice, which is open. The Gm or L group in each population are withdrawn for one period each of Pe and E, giving an La allocation of two periods.

4 CA is not integrated and is arranged in four distinct areas: CDT, Mu, A, Hk/Nk. This reflects the physical layout. First term in year 3 is spent in rotating groups: thereafter each pupil selects two of the four areas in which to work. Thus Mu and A are not 13–16 core curriculum elements, but A may be an implicit aspect of subjects selected. Dr is part of E in year 3, and thereafter an option within CA if staffing permits.

5 Social and Religious Studies (SRS) in years 4 and 5 deals with drugs, poverty, religion, community, etc. Topic-based, with an optional examination output.

6 World Studies (Ws) includes, in year 3, courses in history, geography and politics/economics/sociology for all pupils. In years 4 and 5, pupils choose any *two* of H, G and Bi (British Industrial Society) to O level or CSE. Bi is an AEB Mode 1 syllabus, covering such topics as: small businesses, international companies, labour relations, profit, demand and supply, private and public sectors, government control, wealth distribution, and the social consequences of business activities.

7 S in third year is a school-devised integrated course. In years 4 and 5, pupils may choose to do *either* a double science course with a single CA subject, *or* a single science course with a double CA weighting. Thus S and CA work in effect as a combined option across the year and the two populations. Double subject science may be SCISP, to O level or CSE, or two subject combinations; P + C, or B + C. Single subject science may be either Mode 3 CSE integrated science, or any one of P, B, C (to O level or CSE). In 1981, of the 360 pupils in year 4, 134 chose to do double science (thus the distribution between the two populations in years 4, 5 may not always be equal). Of these, seventeen did P + C, 23 B + C, and the remainder (94) SCISP, which is taught in mixed ability groups; staff consider MAT enhances pupil performance. (Nuffield P is used at A level, but traditional B and C).

Feeder middle schools use either Nuffield Combined Science or the Wreake Valley course.

8 Statistics to O level is available as an extra, using 'twilight' time, on a selective basis.

9 This scheme offers a normal maximum of 10 examination courses to 16 plus, with a possible 12 by adding statistics and English Literature (top E sets). An average student would pursue 9 courses, taking 7 of these to exam level.

10 Alternative non-linguistic courses are offered within the Languages faculty, including a third CA subject, Rs, extra M and E, and Tr as a CSE course.

2 Is the time allocation to a foreign language (two periods of 70 minutes) too low, and are the periods of convenient length?

3 Science is mixed ability 13–16, but mathematics is setted from the first half term. Can both be right?

4 Does Ws sustain adequate experience in history over the years 13–16?

5 Does SRS appear to be a grouping of compatible subjects and topics?

6 Is the provision of a second language at the expense of part of the E and Pe provision satisfactory?

7 There are no separate remedial forms – only remedial groups in E and Ws. Is this adequate provision for slower pupils?

8 Able pupils cannot take three separate science subjects. Are they adequately stretched?

9 Is there too much diversity of choice between science subjects?

10 Is there adequate choice within the curriculum for years 4, 5?

11 Does the single period for SRS in years 4 and 5 represent an adequate provision for those taking it as an exam subject?

12 Is two periods per week in years 4 and 5 adequate for M?

13 Does this curriculum more closely resemble Example A or Example B in *A View of the Curriculum*?

Comments on questions

1 The CA provision has to make the best of separated and cramped buildings, and has evolved from a tradition of separate subject components. It is essentially on Munn lines, and amounts to a choice between separate subjects (not all of which have been listed on the diagram, for the sake of clarity). But the intention throughout has to been to seek some coherent techno-aesthetic provision, and to make Design a central and dominating element,

albeit by means of a separate subject provision because of the constraints indicated. It should also be noted that 13–18 schools have a problem here, since CA provision in middle schools can be patchy. The 11–16 school is perhaps at an advantage – although the advantage is not always taken.

2 The usual allocation is four periods of 35 minutes, and some linguists would regard two periods of 70 minutes as of greater value; others prefer the 'constant drip' of a short daily period if possible. The Berkeley Vale provision (225 minutes) is a notably generous one. My own experience suggests that two 70 minute periods should be enough.

It should be noted that the separation of buildings at Carisbrooke was a most important factor in the school's repeated confirmation of 70 minutes for period length. Although considerations of curriculum design and educational intent were always present, so also was this practical factor.

3 It is never possible to determine whether a curriculum decision is right: only whether it is defensible. At Carisbrooke only mathematics and French are setted from November in year 3, and plainly this reflects the approach of the staff concerned in these subjects. (M. Reid *et al.*, 1981, shows that these two subjects are commonly setted, but not universally so; and presents the practical experience of teachers using mixed ability teaching for both of them.) It is interesting that SCISP (as at Kingshill School) is taught mixed ability, 13–16. This may reflect the liberating effect of integrated science concepts as well as staff attitudes.

It should be noted that mixed ability teaching might be a matter of school policy, as at Sheredes School, because of the moral issues discussed in Chapter 2. But curriculum decisions are essentially decisions about practice, and must always be tempered by what is possible. The position will be different in a school adapting from itself, from that in a school building its staff as it grows from scratch.

4 In years 4 and 5, Ws is taught on a subject basis with an emphasis on a common core of political education. Bi was added to the course at the suggestion of the faculty teaching Ws, and it can be argued that it provides experience in history skills like sifting evidence. It also chimes with the DES interest in the world of industry. But it is an option and not a core element. A greater degree of integration here might give more extensive common ground 13–16 between H and G as core experiences for all pupils. Ws is roughly analogous to a Hu course in some other core curriculum schemes.

5   The SRS faculty is an interesting innovation and a neat way of dealing with Re (so often an isolated subject), Se (often inadequately treated) and Ca (often an isolated period or – as part of DFL programmes – an unrelated item in a patchwork of odds and ends). SRS is also linked with school assemblies. It clearly functions as a very satisfactory core curriculum component at Carisbrooke (see also note 11 below).

6   This seems to me a better solution to this problem than many. It cannot be argued that E or Pe are being downgraded, since both are accepted core subjects 11–16, and neither is dropped by pupils taking the second foreign language. It should be noted that these do not form a top set: they are a self-selected group who may come from any of the mixed-ability English groups.

7   Remedial provision may be concentrated in a separate remedial stream or form – as in many comprehensives – or instead made available, as here, to pupils who remain within the mainstream of curriculum provision. Schools committed to an effective common curriculum seem, not surprisingly, to prefer the latter method of resource allocation and find it effective. This is another issue on which HMI seems unable to make up its mind, and as a result it is inadequately discussed in recent documents. The Carisbrooke provision amounted to the equivalent of nearly three full-time teachers devoted to remedial work.

8   There is no evidence to suggest SCISP is an unsatisfactory basis for A level work. Carisbrooke sends three or four students to Oxbridge every year, and science is well represented. In any event, it does not follow that spending more time on science (or any subject, for that matter) necessarily means more intellectual demands made on pupils. The evidence is that most science teaching is dominated by facts rather than ideas. Spending 20 per cent of the week on science can be a perfectly adequate basis for a stimulating programme.

9   Support at Carisbrooke for SCISP and its single-subject Mode 3 equivalent has grown steadily since it was introduced. The school sees the eventual supplanting of the traditional B, C, P courses by integrated courses as an inevitability – but it is a matter of time. The growing reputation of SCISP-type courses is shifting public opinion in their favour.

10   At first sight, it looks as if the entire curriculum is a rigid common core, with no options. But there are really four option pools, essentially covering CA, S, Hu (as Ws) and La (with its alternatives).

11   Entry to the CSE in SRS is optional, and not confined to the

most able. Only 30 per cent of the marks were awarded to the written paper: the remainder to course work, which all pupils are required to do anyway. This Mode 3 CSE is of interest because it takes a broad view of its subject matter, and has been validated by the humanities, rather than the religious education, panel of the CSE board concerned. It is worth quoting the preamble to the syllabus, since it indicates the questions schools must resolve in developing examined programmes in this area of the curriculum:

i   This syllabus is designed for those schools where:
   a Religious education as a statutory obligation is allied to or interwoven with education on moral, social and health issues;
   b A maximum of 2 single or 1 double period may be expected to be available for the pupils at fourth and fifth year level;
   c Some or all of the teachers involved do not themselves teach from a standpoint of faith or do not necessarily expect to teach the religious aspects of matters of social or individual concern;
   d There is separate provision for a Religious Studies course to be taken to examination level.
ii   The approach [makes] . . . provision for certain topics to be studied without necessarily being related to Christian or other religious principles . . .

The heart of the examination – and of the course in SRS – is the 'production of written essays or other project work on 7 topics chosen from the following lists':

At least 3 from:
The needs of the elderly
*Alcohol and other drugs
Civil rights, liberties and responsibilities
Immigrant groups in society
*World poverty and the underprivileged
*Voluntary and statutory social welfare
The needs of children
The problems of violence
*Love, marriage and sexual relationships
Medical ethics
Conservation and pollution
The effects of mass media
*The world of employment

At least 3 from:
The teachings of Christ
Christian doctrine about the Cross and the Resurrection
*The life of Jesus
Worship
*A major world religion
*Religious festivals
The life of a great religious person
Primitive religions
*Superstition and the supernatural
Religion and the arts
Religious broadcasting
The study of a biblical book or character
Religious scriptures

(Topics marked with an asterisk are always a component of the course.)

It will be seen that, at Carisbrooke, the Ws and SRS programmes interlock in making provision for work in the humanities area. All the topics on both lists could, in fact, arise as part of an 11–16 humanities course for all pupils which interrelated English, geography, history and religious education, and which – by virtue of its learning organisation – incorporated experiences in personal, social and moral education. Such a course might well operate alongside an expressive arts provision which made use of drama 11–16 as a core element. The Carisbrooke approach is an alternative which takes as its focus not the subjects and the broad themes which emerge from subjects in an interrelated humanities course, but specific topics which mark out particular concerns in an extensive territory.

12   Many mathematics teachers would regard this as a minimal provision, particularly when offered as two double periods. But just as the common curriculum reveals unexpected talents in pupils, so also it can reveal unexpected capability and flexibility in staff. In fact, the Carisbrooke mathematics staff were offered more time after experience with the provision, but declined it.

13   It seems to me about halfway between the two. Its two integrated areas – a characteristic of Example B – are Ws and SRS, and of the two SRS is more developed in this sense. But Ws does guarantee core experiences (e.g. political education) which transcend subjects. On the other hand, the rest of the curriculum follows Munn lines, like Example A, and reduces to choices

between subjects. However, it is clear that the Munn caveats about subjects becoming too dominant are well understood at Carisbrooke, and it must be regarded as an outstanding example of an ingenious and extensive common curriculum which triumphs over difficulties, sustains high staff and pupil morale (and performance) and which successfully challenges traditional assumptions – assumptions which, in so many schools, are taken for granted and thus form a barrier to effective curriculum innovation. If I had to mention any doubts, I would name two. First, CA in years 4,5 requires the pupil to choose between an expressive or a techno-aesthetic subject; I should like to see both as core elements, preferably on a unified basis. And second, Ws requires a choice of two subjects from three, when there is a good case for sustaining some aspects of all three. The solution in both cases could only be found by greater integration, and possibly some reallocation of time (perhaps involving a fresh consideration of languages). Such a solution would, of course, push the structure into an Example B form.

But the reality of this curriculum is most impressive and is all the more remarkable for having been established in a school already functioning on a traditional core-plus-options model. There is much to be learnt from studying this structure.

Further reading

Briault, E. and Smith, F. (1980), *Falling Rolls in Secondary Schools*, NFER (Carisbrooke appears as 'Keats' in this study: see esp. part 2, pp. 392–5).

Cornall, P. (1981), 'Case study 11: Carisbrooke School', in E. Henderson and G. Perry (eds), *Change and Development in Schools*, McGraw-Hill.

Cornall, P. (1981), 'Curriculum, timetable and moral judgments', *New Universities Quarterly*, spring.

3   Gillott's School, Henley-on-Thames, Oxfordshire

This is an established mixed 11–16 comprehensive school undergoing a severe reduction in size brought about by the declining birth rate. From a total of 1100 pupils in 1980 as a 7/8 form entry school, numbers will fall to an estimated 760 by 1985: a reduction of 30 per cent over five years, to a 4 form entry school. The total staffing of 60 will fall to about 43, and the number of points available for posts of responsibility from 64 to about 45.

A new head (David Grubb) was appointed in September 1980. In January 1981, his paper 'Falling rolls: Defining the decline, implications and management strategy' set out for staff the national context: the secondary school population will decline by one-third by 1991. Particular implications mentioned were:

staffing: subjects offered, scales awarded, the changing pupil roll influencing the actual teaching role;

classes: how the pupil-teacher ratio is worked out, how we group classes, the size of the core curriculum;

options: how we justify the levels of pressure these exert on the whole school;

pastoral, heads of department: how the pastoral role is to change with fewer pupils and reduced scales, similarly the role of HODs;

scales, points, capitation: how to plan for the decline with systems that have grown with expansion;

senior management: how to manage the pupil decline, what delegation to extend or withdraw;

resources: how to retain equipment, plant, skills, morale;

standards: how to maintain and improve performance;

size: how to rediscover and promote the ethos of the smaller school.

The paper outlined some general strategies and was followed by a day conference and extensive departmental discussion. This resulted in a second paper, 'A faculty based core curriculum model', the following May. This is displayed in the diagram. Finally, in August 1981, the 'Practical assessment and management strategy discussion document' was circulated, which included a paper by the LEA adviser for curriculum and falling rolls on 'Points and declining rolls', costing proposed new scale structures and projecting likely staffing needs. This paper referred to the various visits and in-service activities which had taken place, identified 'areas for specific study', summarised some results from the HMI *Review of Progress* on the Red Book (see Chapter 1), and discussed further the need to move to a faculty structure, the eight faculties – E, M, Hu, Pe, S, La, CA and 'General' (Re and Ca) – pairing where necessary into the five 'frames' listed in note 10 to Figure 3.4.

Year 1	E_6	M_6	Pe_4		Re_2	S_6	Cr_8	H_2	G_2	La_4
Year 2	E_6	M_6	Pe_4		Re_2	S_6	Cr_8	H_2	G_2	La_4
Year 3	E_6	M_6	Pe_4		Re_2	S_6	Cr_8	H_2	G_2	La_4
Year 4	E_6	M_6	Pe_2	La_4	Re_2	S_4	Cr_4	$\left[\begin{smallmatrix}H\\G\end{smallmatrix}\right]_4$	$(Op\ A)_4$	$(Op\ B)_4$
Year 5	E_6	M_6	Pe_2	La_4	Re_2	S_4	Cr_4	$\left[\begin{smallmatrix}H\\G\end{smallmatrix}\right]_4$	$(Op\ A)_4$	$(Op\ B)_4$

*Figure 3.4 Proposed Gillott's School curriculum structure**

Notes
* This condensed display does not show individual forms, since the curriculum is common across each year. It should be noted that this structure is proposed for a period during which numbers in each year will decline from seven to four forms of entry approximately.
1 This assumes 40 periods of 35 minutes weekly.
2 Cr includes art (with photography), crafts and music.
3 Express groups are planned in La, M and for Cs within E.
4 La makes use of the Oxfordshire graded tests scheme and would include Eu as a non-linguistic option.
5 From year 3 on, M would include Cp.
6 In years 4 and 5, S would include Ty or Cd as alternatives to conventional science subjects.
7 In years 4 and 5, options A and B would include a range of subjects, in particular additional science and craft as well as H and G.
8 L and Gm would be offered as second foreign languages as follows. Four periods for L would take place four mornings a week, in place of registration/pastoral: one period for Gm would be found on the fifth morning, along with two from Pe and one during lunch in year 3, and one from Pe and two during lunch in years 4, 5. L and Gm pupils would still be able to attend year assemblies.
9 Ca provision is under discussion and would be incorporated within this model – possibly by revised time allocations or teaching changes within faculties.
10 Five 'faculty frames', initially for timetabling rather than curriculum reasons, are proposed: E/M, Hu (H + G), Pe/S, Cr, F/Re/Ca.

The arguments given in support of a move towards a faculty-based common curriculum and away from the traditional subject-bound curriculum are that the new scheme will be:

(a) more in tune with current core curriculum concepts;
(b) designed to give greater control over class size and forms of pupil grouping;

(c)   designed to provide greater flexibility through a faculty structure that will prove useful in facing pupil number decline and curriculum adaptations.

It is recognised from the beginning that the new curriculum will have far-reaching implications and change established patterns. In the past, for instance, L and Gm have been dependent on heavy 'raiding' on Mu, Re, E, Pe, Cr to provide the necessary periods. The contingency of falling rolls has exposed the underlying assumptions and led to a rather different solution, under which no subjects are dropped, access can be open to all who show interest and L and Gm can be dropped if wished without disrupting pupil programmes. Leaving the existing curriculum intact as rolls fall can result only in a series of expediencies. The new curriculum offers better educational opportunities to pupils and better career development to staff. Either course of action means difficult decisions: but the latter course means decisions which are fundamentally more tractable and more in keeping with a creative role for staff. Three 'main areas for work' are specified:

for *senior staff*, a system to facilitate policy-making;

for *heads of department*, the need to see the role in terms of middle management as well as subject specialisms;

in *curriculum*, to make the issues a matter for constant discussion and assessment among all colleagues.

The proposed structure is based, deliberately, on Example A from *A View of the Curriculum*. This confirms the suggestion advanced in Chapter 1 that, for schools seeking to fashion a common curriculum from a traditional, strongly marked subject-based curriculum, Example A – the Munn model – will be attractive. It should, though, be noted that the proposed curriculum – as is proper for a draft scheme – has yet to be fleshed out, and offers scope in the longer term for integration in a number of faculties (e.g. S, Cr, Hu). This inherent adaptability is an attribute to look for in core curriculum schemes. It should also be noted that the head stresses the need to provide 'some room for local flexibility' within a general, national framework like Example A and the eight 'areas of experience'. 'What we do within the eight areas may depend upon a school and its environment at a certain time.'

The following exercise draws attention to some aspects of the proposal which are worth reflecting upon.

Exercise 8: proposed Gillott's School curriculum

1   Mu appears to stop after year 3, and Dr is presumably part of E. Are the expressive arts adequately covered, 11–16?
2   La is sustained 11–16 as a core element (with some Eu). Can this bold emphasis on La be justified?
3   If S is seen in terms of P, B, C with no integration, some pupils may want to take all three subjects (one in the core, one in each of Op A and Op B). Is this desirable?
4   Hu is on a subject basis as proposed here. Thus H is not a guaranteed core element, and neither are political, social and health education 11–16. Could the treatment of the core components, as taught, be modified to overcome this? Would integration between H and G offer advantages?
5   The time allocation for M is considerable (50 per cent more in years 4 and 5 than that at Carisbrooke). Does the inclusion of computer studies justify this? Should Cp be closely identified with M in the curriculum?
6   E is a separate subject with a substantial time allocation. How might it be treated as a core element? Should links be forged with other elements in the core?

4   Holsworthy School, Devon

This is a four form entry mixed 11–16 comprehensive school serving a rural area. Upon reorganisation (from a secondary modern school) in 1976, the curriculum in years 1–3 followed conventional lines, and that for years 4 and 5 combined a larger core with four option pools (Figure 3.5).

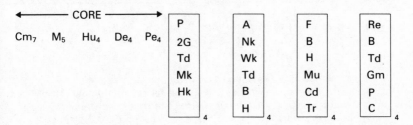

Figure 3.5

A number of difficulties arose from the workings of this option system in a small comprehensive. Some individual pupil choices gave programmes which lacked balance; more able students evidently had more choice; and providing enough different choices in the pools absorbed staff time.

An extensive series of staff discussions began. As a general philosophy, it was agreed that 'This educational community seeks to provide a happy and stable environment in which all who are a part of it can be helped to develop their full potential. We seek to develop respect for and understanding of self, other people and the environment.' Further reflection led to growing interest in the notion of a common curriculum, and by 1980 a document 'The pentamerous curriculum', outlining a five-sided core with two option pools in years 4 and 5, had been prepared by the head and deputy (Malcolm Woodward and Jack Marsh), with additional papers on faculty structures by the relevant staff. This model was agreed with staff, governors and parents, and implemented for the fourth year pupils in September 1981.

Meanwhile, staff discussion has continued on the form of the common curriculum in years1–3, and the agreed scheme for years 4 and 5 has been used to reshape the curriculum in the earlier years.

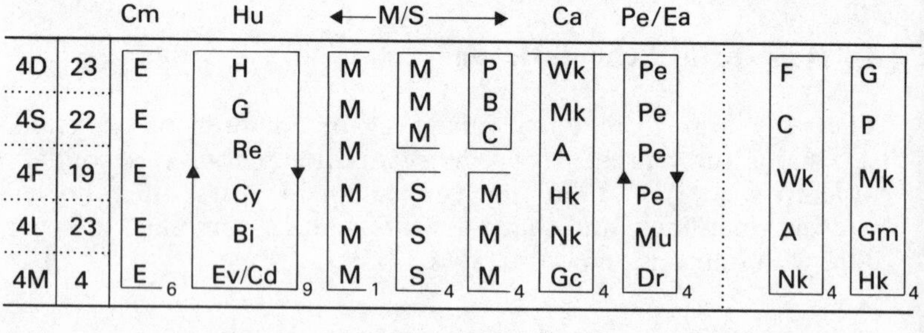

Figure 3.6 Holsworthy Curriculum Structure: year 4.

Notes

1 4L is a remedial group, integrated within the curriculum.
2 The core Hu course (which includes Ca) takes a minimum of three periods, leaving six for subject choice. Able pupils (by taking Cy as a result of core work) can obtain three subjects (e.g. Cy, Bi, G) as 16-plus exams from the total Hu provision. Less able pupils spend six periods on the Hu core and take a single subject to exam level.

3 This small school has only one specialist in each of B, C and P. For M and S, therefore, the year group is split into two populations, one rather abler than the other. Co-operation between M and S allows setting. Note that one period of M is, however, setted across the whole year. All pupils in the less able population take applied science (Mode 3 CSE) instead of the separate subjects.

4 The Pe/Ea faculty has the whole year for one afternoon. In the first term Mu, Dr, Pe are offered in rotation. Thereafter the course becomes modular, with a Pe element retained and pupils choosing two broad areas each linked on a thematic basis.

5 CA (Creative studies) is an integrated course linking Wk, Mk, A, Nk and Gc. Pupils opt for either 'design-based' or 'arts-based' courses emphasising the creative/constructional or the expressive respectively. O level and CSE exams are taken in separate subjects and a Mode 3 CSE, wholly assessed in terms of course work, is currently under way.

The intention is that the five core areas – M/S, Cm, Hu, CA and Pe/Ea – should constitute the total curriculum in each of years 1, 2 and 3. The process of adjustment has already begun and will be taken further each successive year. Thus 1st year Hu uses a thematic approach to study 'The origin of the Earth', linking H, G, Re, E and Ev. In years 2 and 3, E is separated and Hu becomes separate H, G and Re, each for 2 periods weekly. A core Hu element returns in years 4 and 5. CA in years 1–3 is an integrated course in De for all, and in years 1 and 2 the Cm team combines with E, Mu and Dr staff to offer an Ea course developed pragmatically from a variety of starting points, e.g. visits to dark forest (mystery) and Dartmoor (contrasts), or 'The Stone Wall' (mini opera by Malcolm Williamson) (war and peace).

On the other hand, S in years 1 and 2 has yet to be blocked across the year or half year: it is hoped that some rationalisation of laboratory equipment and courses will allow this. Closer links may develop between E, F and Gm as part of the Cm faculty. The model on which the core curriculum in years 1–3 is based may be represented as in Table 3.2.

TABLE 3.2

Faculty	Core	Associated elements/options
M/S	M, Cp, B, C, P	S extension, Cp extension
Cm	E (language and literature)	F, Gm
Hu	Core experience	H, G, Re, Ev, Bi, Cd
CA	De core	A, Mk, Nk, Wk, Hk, Gc
Pe/Ea	Mu, Dr, Pe, Ga	School games, band, dance club, choir, instrumental, productions

Summary

The isolated position of this small school (565 on roll) means that the task of packing a core curriculum into the school day is particularly difficult. The two key elements are plainly a clear understanding of educational purpose, and the closest involvement of all staff in curriculum design and implementation. A traditional subject-based curriculum had become firmly embedded in many areas: a notable exception was in CA where a new building gave a fillip to team teaching and allowed fresh ideas to blossom. Two points of interest are, first, the strategy of introducing the new curriculum at fourth year level: the theory here was that this tackled the examination hurdle, and once this was overcome there would be no problem extending the ideas throughout the 11–16 curriculum. Second, the extent to which subject integration has been established in Hu, CA and Pe/Ea is worth noting: a considerable achievement in a school very much dependent on its own resources. Further, the new curriculum allows integration to be taken up in other areas in the future – in S, for instance, and possibly Cm. The mature 11–16 curriculum on this model would conform to Example B of *A View of the Curriculum* and make very effective use of the resources of a small school.

Exercise 9: Holsworthy curriculum proposal

1 Ca is part of the Hu core. Are there advantages in this?
2 How might F be linked more closely with E?
3 What are the defensible ways of introducing Gm as the second foreign language?
4 Is it necessary to place any constraints on the choice in Opt A and Opt B to ensure curriculum balance?
5 Assuming unconstrained choice in the options in years 4 and 5, does the core show any evident bias towards a particular curriculum component?
6 What time allocations would you recommend to the five faculties for the proposed curriculum in years 1–3?
7 If resources allowed, what additional subject inputs would you like to see in the core curriculum, and in the options?
8 What are the implications of the proposed curriculum structure for teaching styles and learning strategies? Are there implications for pupil grouping?

Further reading

Marsh, J. (1981), 'An answer to falling rolls?', *The Times Educational Supplement*, 23 October (article describing the origins and form of the Holsworthy School curriculum).

5   Kingshill School, Cirencester, Gloucestershire

This is a 4 form entry mixed 11–16 comprehensive school which serves a mainly – though not exclusively – rural area. It opened as a purpose-built comprehensive with first year pupils only in September 1976; the head (Keith Greenwood) had been appointed the previous January and started to plan the curriculum 'with some concept of the curriculum as a whole'. Originally, the school was to have a third phase of building taking it to six forms of entry, but this has been dropped. The accommodation is therefore unbalanced in some areas: there is only one small Wk room and one small Mk room. The school is building its own extension to include provision for Cp, making use in part of funds raised by parents.

The school's common curriculum owes much to the philosophy that 'children – and adults – are capable of far more than we give them credit for'. But it owes much, too, to the establishment of a climate in which staff are encouraged to exploit the potential of all pupils, and to a style of curriculum change which makes use in a pragmatic way of the talents of staff and of their success in building the curriculum as the first pupils moved up the school. 'Change isn't as difficult as people make out. Staff don't necessarily arrive with the views you want, but once the set up of the school, and its general approach to the curriculum have been established, they respond.' The curriculum was put first, with examinations its servant: 'We were determined to do work we considered valuable and appropriate. Then we found exams which suited the work, or developed our own.'

Innovation, however, must be acceptable to parents and governors as well as to staff, and the same pragmatic approach was adopted in coping with the political aspects of curriculum change. An important curriculum element is English Studies (ES), and the head of this faculty is an English specialist. But it is organised in years 1–3 as a coherent course using specialists in H and G: it is, in effect, an integrated Hu course which also incorporates Dr.

137

Case studies and school decisions

1A	24	ES	F_3	Re_1	M_4	S_3	Pe_2	Mu_1	A/Cr_3		
1B	25	ES	"	"	"	"	"	"	"		
1C	24	ES	"	"	"	"	"	"	"		
1D	23	ES	"	"	"	"	"	"	"		
1E	24	ES	"	"	"	"	"	"	"		

$[ES]_8$ $[Rm]_{12}$ $[Rm]_5$

2A	25	ES	F	Re_1	M	S_3	Pe_2	Mu_1	A_1	Cr_2	
2B	26	ES	F	"	M	"	"	"	"	"	
2C	24	ES	F	"	M	"	"	"	"	"	
2D	27	ES	F	"	M	"	"	"	"	"	
2E	25	ES	F	"	M	"	"	"	"	"	

$[ES]_8$ $[Rm]_7$ $[F]_3$ $[M]_4$

3A	26	ES_6	Gm_2	F_2	M	Ca_1	Re_1	S_3	A_1	Cr_2	Pe_2	Mu_1
3B	26	ES		F	M	"	"	"	"	"	"	"
3C	27	ES		F	M	"	"	"	"	"	"	"
3D	26	ES		F	M	"	"	"	"	"	"	"
3E	26	ES		F	M	"	"	"	"	"	"	"

$[ES]_7$ $[Rm]_7$ $[F]_3$ $[M]_4$

								Opt A	Opt B
4A	26	E	Hu	F	P	M	Ga	2B	C
4B	26	E	Hu	F	S	M	Ga	Mk	P
4C	25	E	Hu	F	S	M	Ga	Wk	4Cr
4D	27	E	Hu	F	S	M	Ga	Hk	A/Nk
4E	26	E	Hu	Gm	S	M	Ga	Gm	G

$[E]_4$ $[Hu]_3$ $[F/Gm]_3$ $[S]_3$ $[M]_4$ $[Ga]_2$

Opt A: 2B, Mk, Wk, Hk, Gm, Cp, H, Td — subscript 3
Opt B: C, P, 4Cr, A/Nk, G — subscript 3

5A	25	E	Hu	F	P	M	Ga	C	2B
5B	26	E	Hu	F	S	M	Ga	Td	Mk
5C	24	E	Hu	F	S	M	Ga	4Cr	Wk
5D	26	E	Hu	F	S	M	Ga	PA	Hk
5E	25	E	Hu	Gm	S	M	Ga	A	Gm

$[E]_4$ $[Hu]_3$ $[F/Gm]_3$ $[S]_3$ $[M]_4$ $[Ga]_2$

Col 1: C, Td, 4Cr, PA, A — subscript 3
Col 2: 2B, Mk, Wk, Hk, Gm, Td — subscript 3

Figure 3.7 Kingshill curriculum structure

Notes

1 There are 25 periods of one hour each week. In each year, the four forms of entry are arranged into five form groups.
2 ES is a team-taught Hu-style course comprising E, H, G and including one weekly period of Dr.
3 The same teacher takes M and S for each first year form.
4 S in years 1 and 2 is Nuffield Combined. In year 3, separate P, C, B. In years 4 and 5, one top set of 28 takes P; the remainder take integrated science as a single subject (Mode 3 CSE).
5 Pupils who take Gm in year 3 are identified as likely to benefit in light of F and E performance. These lose one period each of ES, F.
6 In years 4 and 5, pupils who began Gm in year 3 take Gm in Opt A/B. Gm is also available instead of F to less able pupils in the La core.
7 In years 4 and 5, E and Hu are staffed separately. There is some setting for Eng. lit. only. E and Hu continue to work closely together.
8 The suggestion of ultimately bringing Re within ES in years 2 and 3 is being considered. In years 4 and 5, Re is part of E.
9 In years 4 and 5, Ca is taken as needed from M.
10 *Examinations*: O level F and Gm are Mode 1, but CSE F is Mode 3 and consortium based, with large oral element. General (integrated) S Mode 3 is topic-based CSE. All pupils take Hu in fourth and fifth core, leading for many to JMB Mode 1 O level Integrated Humanities (100 per cent course work) or to a parallel Mode 3 CSE, for which the CSE board requires an examined component.

Similarly, the success of the La faculty in teaching F effectively to all pupils (except for a very few, an odd pupil or two in each year, who go instead for remedial help) has led to its incorporation as a core element in years 4 and 5. This is acceptable to pupils: 'because they don't choose it, they don't think in terms of dropping it'. Graded tests in F are used over years 1 to 5 (the SW regional system).

The same thinking lies behind the organisation of S in years 4 and 5. A SCISP double-subject programme was likely to be at least partially unacceptable within the school's constituency. Instead, all pupils except a top set of twenty-eight take a school-based integrated science CSE of marked originality, and additional traditional subjects are available in the option groups. Forming the top P set runs counter to the mixed-ability approach within science, but it ensures that the ablest pupils can take the three separate sciences without distorting the curriculum for the rest. An incidental advantage is that there is no tendency for girls to drop science.

The S and ES faculties are of particular interest. The S approach for all five years is not to begin with concepts and then hope to find applications, but to ask 'Where does science manifest itself in the world?' and work backwards to concepts. The CSE course consists of five modules: industrial science (e.g. plastics), transport (e.g. lubrication), energy, communication technology (e.g. reprographics), and food and health (e.g. ecology). 40 per cent of the marks are course work-based.

The ES faculty work is resource based and shows considerable innovation in its design and implementation. It is, like S, taught mixed ability for all five years (apart from some Eng. Lit. setting) and thematically organised. The themes from which the fourth and fifth year work is composed are: law and order; people and work; mass media; consumer affairs; education; the family, persecution and prejudice; poverty; the community; war. O level candidates take AEB Syllabus 11; CSE are assessed on course work. In O level (lit. only) 60 per cent of the marks are course work-based.

Summary

This is a most interesting and inventive common curriculum programme which makes maximum use of resources and overcomes some awkward problems arising from the school's small size and lack of CDT facilities. The latter prevent a common core design programme (cf. Holsworthy School), but all pupils do A/Cr in years 1–3 (no gender split) and virtually all will choose at least one Cr or A subject in years 4 and 5 from the two options. A second foreign language is introduced by 'raiding' two kindred activities – E and F – and there seems some rough justice in this solution. The compulsory P set for abler pupils in years 4 and 5 is an unusual but ingenious solution which takes account of both educational ideals and political realities. Separate subjects are extensively taught as such in years 1–3, which again reflects a compromise between the school's common core philosophy and the practicalities of what is possible on the ground.

An interesting aspect of the ES faculty is the way in which it shows how a Hu programme can be used to cover not only work in E, H and G, but also that corpus of 'life skills' which is often labelled 'personal and social development' and hived off into a separate area or into a DFL course. The core La programme is unusual but is an example of organic growth: it might be difficult to institute it within an established school. *In toto*, the scheme lies somewhere between Examples A and B; there are aspects of both.

If it were possible to establish a core CA/De area, it would be a pure Example B structure. As it is, it offers a great deal of interest to curriculum designers and it is worth mentioning that the examination results of the school's first pupils in summer 1981 were particularly pleasing. Of 133 pupils in the fifth year – all entered for public examinations – 91 per cent obtained 5 or more graded passes, and 25 per cent of these were at higher grades (ABC O level, CSE 1). Performance in science – which is organised mixed-ability 11–16 – was especially good.

Exercise 10: Kingshill School

1 What are the arguments for and against La as an 11–16 core element?
2 Are there alternative ways of introducing Gm in year 3?
3 Assuming adequate facilities, how might the scheme be altered to introduce CA/De as a core element?
4 Mu is a single period in years 1–3, and then is discontinued (except as an off-timetable extra). What alternative arrangements might be devised?
5 Dr is a part of ES, and there are plans to incorporate Re too. Are these desirable developments?
6 Examine the time allocations to the various subjects and faculties. Is there evidence of imbalance?
7 Does the provision for Ca seem satisfactory?
8 What are the virtues and snags in the S programme, 11–16?

6 Priory School, Weston-super-Mare, Avon

This is a 7/8 form entry mixed comprehensive school which opened in new buildings in September 1975. It operates currently as an 11–16 school but may become 11–18 in the future.

The curriculum display shows how every component of the timetable is blocked, and, as at Berkeley Vale School, the basic modules are consistently repeated. The head of Priory School (Arthur Spencer) developed this consistent blocking technique when deputy at Castle School, Thornbury, Bristol: the deputy at Berkeley Vale (Michael Hardwick) was formerly at Castle School. These techniques vastly reduce the labour of timetabling. There are seven faculties: Ca, E, Hu, M, La, S and Se (which includes Pe). It will be noted that the time allocations to each are very

Faculty: E Hu La M S Ca ◄——Se——►

Block 1

Row	No.	E	Hu	La	M	S	Ca			Se
1.1	26	E	Hu	F	M	S	2A	Pe	Ga	Se
1.2	26	E	Hu	F	M	S	2Mu	Pe	Ga	Se
1.3	27	E	Hu	F	M	S	Wk	Pe	Ga	Se
1.4	24	E	Hu	F	M	S	Mk	Pe	Ga	Se
1.5	25	E	Hu	F	M	S	Nk	Pe	Ga	Se
1.6	25	E	Hu	F	M	S	Po	Pe	Ga	Se
1.7	24	E	Hu	F	M	S		Pe	Ga	Se
1.8	26	E_3	Hu_3	$F_{2.5}$	M_3	$S_{2.5}$	$2Hk_3$	Pe_1	Ga_1	Se_1

Block 2

Row	No.	E	Hu	La	M	S	Ca			Se
2.1	29	E	Hu	F	M	S	2A	Pe	Ga	Se
2.2	29	E	Hu	2F	M	S	2Mu	Pe	Ga	Se
2.3	28	E	Hu		M	S	Wk	Pe	Ga	Se
2.4	27	E	Hu	F	M	S	Mk	Pe	Ga	Se
2.5	26	E	Hu	F	M	S	Nk	Pe	Ga	Se
2.6	28	E	Hu	2F	M	S	Po	Pe	Ga	Se
2.7	27	E	Hu		M	S		Pe	Ga	Se
2.8	26	E_3	Hu_3	$F_{2.5}$	M_3	S_3	$2Hk_3$	Pe_1	Ga_1	$Se_{.5}$

Block 3

Row	No.	E	Hu	La	M	S	Ca			Se
3.1	31	E	Hu	F	M	S	2A	Pe	Ga	Se
3.2	30	E	Hu	F	M	S	2Mu	Pe	Ga	Se
3.3	30	E	Hu	F	M	S	Wk	Pe	Ga	Se
3.4	31	E	Hu	F	M	S	Mk	Pe	Ga	Se
3.5	30	E	Hu	F	M	S	Nk	Pe	Ga	Se
3.6	28	E	Hu	F	M	S	Po	Pe	Ga	Se
3.7	29	E	Hu	F	M	S	2Hk	Pe	Ga	Se
3.8	28	E_3	Hu_3	$F_{2.5}$	$M_{2.5}$	S_3	Td_3	Pe_1	Ga_1	Se_1

Block 4

Row	No.	E	Hu	La	M	S	Ca	Ga	Se	[A]	[B]
4.1	29	E		F	M	2S	3A	Ga	Se	2G	2A
4.2	27	E	3G	F	M	2P	Mk	Ga	Se		Po
4.3	32	E	2H	F	M	2P	Wk	Ga	Se	3Ci	2Hk
4.4	31	E		F	M	B	Nk	Ga	Se	2Pe	Nk
											Je
4.5	32	E		F	M	2P	2Td	Ga	Se	Ls	Td
4.6	30	E	3G	F	M	C	3Hk	Ga	Se	Cs	Mk
4.7	32	E	2H	F	M	B	Mv	Ga	Se		2B
4.8	29	E_3		F_2	M_3	S_2	$2Mu_2$	Ga_1	Se_1	Gm_2	2C / P_2

Block 5

Row	No.	E	Hu	La	M	S	Ca	Ga	Se	[A]	[B]
5.1	30	E		F	M	2P	2A	Ga	Se	G	2C
5.2	28	E	4G	F	M	B	Mk	Ga	Se	H	2B
5.3	30	E	H	F	M	C	Wk	Ga	Se	2Pe	P
5.4	28	E		F	M	S	Nk	Ga	Se	Cy	2Hk
5.5	28	E		F	M	2P	Td	Ga	Se	3Ls	2A
5.6	29	E	3G	F	M	2B	3Hk	Ga	Se	3Ci	Nk
5.7	29	E	2H	F	M		Mv	Ga	Se	Sp	Mv
5.8	30	E_3		F_2	M_3	S_2	Mv_2	Ga_1	Se_1		

Figure 3.8 Priory Curriculum Structure

Notes
1 There are 20 periods weekly, each of 70 minutes.
2 A total of 30 periods is allocated for remedial work.
3 An additional B group in year 4 was originally taught off-timetable, and so was an additional P group in year 5. This is not now available.
4 The blocked timetable enables every faculty to hold a weekly meeting as part of the timetable.
5 There are seven partially hearing pupils, to whom eighteen extra periods are allocated weekly.

similar, which facilitates consistent blocking (though the faculty allocations are not equal, as at Berkeley Vale: and the Priory timetable is a conventional 5-day one). The Special Education Department is not timetabled: remedial provision is by individual withdrawal. There is also a Partially Hearing Unit on site, linked with this department.

Three features of the organisation should be noted before looking at the curriculum. First, the head has fostered staff involvement in curriculum decisions, and placed only two constraints on the staff curriculum committee: that there should be a faculty of Se, and that year tutors and heads of faculties should be at the same scale level. The head normally accepts any recommendations provided they can be justified to the governors and LEA. Second, there is an extensive programme of staff development which includes at least one annual conference. And third, particular stress is laid on guidance, which forms part of the 'pastoral curriculum' pursued by year and form tutors in registration periods and of the Se core course.

A salient feature of the curriculum is the extensive use of mixed ability teaching. Although F is setted after year 1, there is otherwise only a top E set in each half year of years 4 and 5. It will be seen that the curriculum for years 1–3 is virtually identical, and that there is no provision for starting a second foreign language in year 3. This is the simplest solution to this tiresome problem, but should not be overlooked. All pupils take F for all five years, and in year 4 either Gm or Sp is included in Option A – the choice changes from year to year. Graded tests are used throughout the La programme 11–16.

There is a change of gear from years 1–3 into years 4 and 5. Hu is dropped from the core, and becomes a choice between H and G: similarly S is no longer an integrated programme but a choice between B, P, C and S (general science). Pupils may take two

143

foreign languages and a maximum of two science subjects (see note 3 to Figure 3.8). The school is satisfied this raises no careers problems. Throughout years 1–5, staff teams are in general assembled on a half year basis, taking each parallel 4 fe population in turn. The exceptions are Ca and Ga.

Two faculties are of particular interest. The Hu programme in years 1–3 is team taught, resource based and thematically organised around the general concept of 'Exploration'. Thus third year 'topics for investigation' are: exploring cities, exploring people at war, exploring beliefs, and exploring Spaceship Earth. Use is made of Schools Council Integrated Humanities Project materials, and of RLDU materials (which are also used in several other faculties). This inquiry-centred course covers ground in Ec, Re, So and anthropology, archaeology and politics as well as in H and G, and aims to foster interdisciplinary links in studying issues.

The Se faculty runs over the five years 11–16 and offers core experiences in social, moral and health education; careers; Pe, leisure studies, outdoor activities and community service. By taking Ci, Pe, Ls or Cy from Option A in years 4 and 5, the course may be extended and lead to CSE exams in Ci (Mode 1) or Pe (Mode 3). Although Pe and Ga are taught separately from Se, Pe staff are involved in Se, which aims:

to encourage and develop feelings of personal self esteem and self identity;

to encourage the individual to recognise and understand his or her role in society;

to provide the opportunity for the assimilation of a field of knowledge;

to enable the individual to develop his or her social or communicative skills.

For example, the third year programme covers five topics: general rules of decision-making (e.g. buying a home); decision-making exercises (e.g. siting a motorway or oil refinery); careers; education for personal relationships; and health education (smoking, alcohol). Extensive use is made of outside speakers, film and video, links with industry and the community, and team teaching by faculty staff. Summer camps for pupils are also a strongly marked feature.

144

Summary

This is a rationally planned, exceptionally well administered broad-core curriculum 11–16 which offers all pupils a remarkable range of opportunities. A direct link is plainly perceived between a common curriculum and mixed ability teaching (MAT 11–16 in M is particularly unusual). Examination results are especially pleasing, and the proportion of leavers continuing in full-time education is very high.

The structure is essentially a combination of a Munn (Example A) curriculum with a consistently blocked timetable. The result is a highly developed and well unified Munn solution. The core Se programme has benefits, and it is rare to see Pe explicitly involved in He programmes. The core F component is evidently successful. It is, however, arguable that the incorporation of Ea elements within a subject-based CA core may give them inadequate representation over the five years.

Exercise 11: Priory School

1   Is there any overlap between the aims of the Se faculty and the work capable of being undertaken in other faculties? How does the focus of the Se faculty compare with the SRS faculty at Carisbrooke, and ES at Kingshill?

2   Under what circumstances might the Hu programme in years 1–3 be extended to years 4 and 5? Are there aspects of the integrated approach to Hu which could present difficulties if such an extension were planned?*

3   The integrated S in years 1–3 gives way to separate subjects in years 4 and 5. What are the possible reasons for this?

4   If a SCISP-type programme were adopted for S in years 4 and 5, the choice of no more than two separate science subjects would be avoided. Is this desirable? Would there be any advantage in a compromise solution using single subject integrated science, as at Kingshill?

5   Would it be possible, within the existing core structure, to operate an integrated De/CA programme for years 1–5? What are the implications of such a step?

6   Examine the weightings given to the elements of the core curriculum. How are the expressive arts (A, Mu, D) treated over the five years?

7   Justify the place of F as a core element 11–16. Does it exist at the expense of any other important curriculum component?
8   Is it desirable to involve Pe staff within an Se programme? Does this distort the role of Pe staff? Or should the process be taken further, so that Pe and Ga become completely integrated within Se? Might this radically change the nature of traditional Pe?

Further reading

Block 1 of Open University Course E 323 *Approaches to School Management* gives Priory School extensive coverage. Further information is also to be found in the corresponding reader, of the same title, edited by Bush, Glatter, Goodey and Bridges (Harper & Row, 1980).

*It is worth noting that staff wished to extend Hu into years 4 and 5, but could not reconcile this with external examination requirements. Comparison might be made with the solutions devised at Carisbrooke, Kingshill and Sheredes in order to overcome this problem.

7   Sheredes School, Hoddesdon, Hertfordshire

This is a 6 form entry mixed 11–18 comprehensive school serving a semi-urban area. It opened in 1969 with first year pupils only as a 5 fe school. Enlargement to 6 fe was completed in 1978.

A common curriculum was adopted from the beginning, and this school presents the most mature example in these studies (if not

TABLE 3.3

	1979	1980	1981
No. of students in year group	147	150	170
Proportion obtaining 5 or more subjects at higher grades	30%	31%	27%
Proportion obtaining 5 or more subject grades	94	93	94
Average number of subject grades per student	7.3	7.2	7.3

nationally) of a common curriculum structure 11–16. Despite parental choice and other schools nearby offering a traditional curriculum, the intake is fully subscribed and all abilities are fairly represented. Although few of the original staff are now left (the new head, Gertrude Seddon, was appointed in January 1977), the curriculum structure is unchanged, and examination results have reached a consistently high level (Table 3.3).

Some features of school organisation are worth mentioning. The school forum is seen as an important institution for fostering democratic styles of decision making and pupil involvement, and meets weekly at three separate levels: years 1–3, 4–5 and 6–7. The school, although purpose-built as a comprehensive, has been adapted to common curriculum needs with a central resource facility and blocked spaces for each faculty. Decisions are extensively delegated, but elaborate administrative systems are avoided and paperwork kept to a minimum. Informal contact is valued. Pupil records are centrally available and based on regular assessments using written comments.

The curriculum display shows that the seven faculties are blocked by the year and half year, and that MAT is the rule rather than the exception across all five years. In years 4 and 5, M is arranged in each half year into an O level group and 2 parallel CSE groups; S in the core is in four groups – SCISP O level, SCISP CSE, and two parallel single-subject CSE groups. The timetable components are not equal enough in size to permit consistent blocking, but some faculty meetings are possible within the weekly timetable.

The notation is not subtle enough to show variations in the organisation of learning between faculties. Hu is entirely team taught, and integrated in year 1 with the same teacher staying with the form group. Thereafter an interrelated structure is used, with groups rotating between component subjects in a thematically based programme. Subject identities are retained. Ea is similar, but has no explicit examination orientation and there are regular integrated activities built around productions within the half year. Ea is linked with school and year assemblies. M is flexibly grouped with some team teaching. CA is team taught throughout, with common themes underlying a rotating system in years 1 to 3. Thereafter all pupils take an integrated De course, linking A, Cr and Hk/Nk in a series of internal options under the headings Communication; Human aids and extensions; Living and working space. S uses Nuffield Combined in years 1 and 2, SCISP across year 3, and is taught mainly in class groups but with some staff

Faculty:		Hu	Ea	M	CA	Pa		S	La	Opt
1F	29	Hu	E	M	2Mk	Pe	Ga	S	F	
1D	30	Hu	Mu	M	Wk	Pe	Ga	Š	F	
1C	31	Hu	Dr	M	Hk	Pe	Ga	S	F	
					Nk		Ga			
1K	27	Hu	E	M	2A	Pe	Ga	S	F	
1L	29	Hu	Mu	M	Gc	Pe	Ga	S	F	
1A	30	Hu 5	Dr 3	M 3	Po 3	Pe 1	Ga	S 2	F 2	
2B	30	2E	E	M	2Mk	Pe	Ga	S	F	
2P	32	H	Mu	M	Wk	Pe	Ga	S	F	
2C	30	Cs	Dr	M	Nk	Pe	Ga	S	F	
							Ga			
2J	28	G	E	M	Hk	Pe	Ga	S	F	
2N	31	Re	Mu	M	2A	Pe	Ga	S	F	
2R	31	5	Dr 3	M 3	Po 3	Pe 1	Ga 1	S 2	F 2	
3B	29	2E	E	M	2Mk	Pe	Ga	S	F	**Opt A** 2Gm
3Q	30		Mu	M	Wk	Pe	Ga	S	F	L
3M	30	H	Dr	M	Nk	Pe	Ga	S	F	
4J	29	2G	E	M	Hk / 2A	Pe	Ga	S	F	2S
3P	32	Re	Mu	M	Td	Pe	Ga	S	F	3Cr
3Y	32	5	Dr 2	M 2	Po 2	Pe 1	Ga 1	S 3	F 2	A 1

Faculty:		Hu	Ea	M			CA	Pa		S	**Opt B**	**Opt C**
4A	28	2E	E	M		S	De	Pe	Ga		2F	2S
4G	29		Mu	2M		S	De	Pe	Ga		2S	Gm
4M	32		Dr			2S	De	Pe	Ga		Nk	L
		2H					De		Ga		A	Hk
4S	32		E	M		S	De	Pe	Ga		Td	Tk
4L	29	2G	Mu	2M		S	De	Pe	Ga		(Ex)	Re
4E	30	5	Dr 2		3	2S 2	De 2	Pe 1	Ga 1		(T)	Hb
											(Mv)	A
											(Co)	(T)
											Mu 2	2

Faculty:		Hu	Ea	M			CA	Pa		S	Opt B	Opt C
5R	31	2E	E	M		S	De	Pe	Ga		2F	2S
5C	30		Mu	2M		S	De	Pe	Ga		2S	Gm
5M	27		Dr			2S	De	Pe	Ga		Nk	L
		2H					De		Ga		A	Hk
5S	32		E	M		S	De	Pe	Ga		Td	Tk
5W	31		Mu	2M		S	De	Pe	Ga		(Ex)	Re
5K	31	2G 5	Dr 2		2	2S 3	De 2	Pe 1	Ga 1		(T)	A
											(Mv)	Hb
											(Co)	(T)
											Mu 2	2

Figure 3.9   Sheredes curriculum structure

Notes
1 There are 20 periods weekly, each of 70 minutes.
2 Remedial help is by extraction and use of floating teachers, and totals about 40 teacher periods. Withdrawal for E help in year 1 may be from any faculty; thereafter mainly from Hu, and continues decreasingly to year 5. M help mainly by use of floater, years 1–4.
3 Form groups are retained as the basic teaching unit in all faculties except Ca, Pe and Ga. But they are blocked, and there is flexible movement between them.
4 In each of years 4 and 5, there is an off-timetable Gm group.
5 Hu includes Re, Se and some He over years 1–5. Other He in S. Distribution of specialists in Hu teams may vary.
6 Gm and L in Opt A (year 3) open to all. Alternative courses in S, Cr and A (linked with E) are interest based.
7 Extra S to be chosen from either Opt B or C in years 4,5.
8 Ca taken as needed from Hu, M and S in years 4 and 5, and a major tutorial component in year 3.
9 *Examinations*: Hu leads to Mode 3 O level and CSE exams in E (single subject: lang and lit combined), H and G. Mu only from Ea leads to O level, with one off-timetable period. M leads to Mode 1 SMP or equivalent Mode 1 CSE. CA to Mode 3 CSE in De, or AEB Mode 1 O level. La uses Mode 1 F, Gm to O level, CSE; L is Cambridge Classics Project. S as double subject (taking extra S from Opt B or Opt C) leads to SCISP at O level or CSE; S as single subject to Mode 3 CSE in integrated science.

exchanges. Most option subjects lead to O level and CSE. Link courses are with the nearby college of FE, and are paid for from the school staffing allocation, as are all remedial and peripatetic teachers. The overall staffing ratio on this comprehensive basis is 1: 16.1, and the staff contact ratio is 0.781. Distribution of bonus between years 1–5 is virtually even.

This curriculum structure has been evolved from a theory of education with two broad strands. The primary strand is to do with establishing favourable conditions under which learning can occur in a flexible way: hence the emphasis on resource based strategies and a mixed ability format, and on team planning between staff. The secondary strand owes much to Hirst's suggestion that liberal education may be identified with distinct forms of knowledge and understanding. Although this has not directly determined the faculty structure, it has underpinned the approach to the organisation of learning experiences within faculties. Knitting these two strands together to implement the structure is a concept of the curriculum as practical action and the solution of uncertain problems, which is on all fours with the work of Schwab and Reid.

Summary

This is a high-level broad-core programme which corresponds exactly to the outline advanced in Example B of *A View of the Curriculum*. The core in years 4 and 5 takes up 80 per cent of the time and fulfils both a Hirstian prescription for a liberal education, and also more instrumental aims to do with society's needs: e.g. Pe, and Se, Me and He. It should be noted that neither these, nor Ca, are concentrated within a separate faculty; E is an influential component across two faculties (Hu and Ea), and all pupils have an interrelated programme in E, H, G and Re which includes 'life skills' areas. The inclusion of E within Hu is unusual and occurs in only one other of these case studies (Kingshill). But there is no evidence that E performance is anything but enhanced (half of the fifth year group consistently secure a higher grade pass in E; while, in 1981, 68 per cent achieved this in H).

The combination of team teaching, mixed ability organisation and a clear educational philosophy makes this a tightly organised programme in which curriculum and organisation are completely unified, and all pupils are offered a programme which is broad, balanced and coherent within the terms of this philosophy.

Exercise 12: Sheredes School

1 What is the case for linking E, H, G and Re within a Hu faculty around a weak thesis of integration, as here? What might be the advantages of using a stronger thesis, as at Priory?

2 What are the virtues and snags in making E a component of two faculties, rather than a free-standing subject in its own right?

3 Pupils wishing to take SCISP (double science) and two languages must take Gm in twilight time (two after-school periods). What are the alternatives to this? What, in any event, is the case for taking more than one foreign language 11–16?

4 Examine the scheme for beginning Gm or L in year 3. How does it compare with other solutions in these studies?

5 Are the arrangements for providing Se, He Me and Ca within the faculties likely to be adequate?

6 All pupils take De in years 4 and 5. Examine the time allocations to the various curriculum areas and consider

whether this requirement constrains any others.
7 Assume that there is a case for making a foreign language compulsory 11–16. Examine ways in which this scheme might be modified to allow for this, and consider carefully the effect its introduction would have on the breadth and balance of the existing scheme.

Further reading

Holt, M. (1976), 'Curriculum development at Sheredes School', in J Walton and J Welton (eds), *Rational Curriculum Planning*, Ward Lock Educational.
Holt, M. (1978), *The Common Curriculum*, Routledge & Kegan Paul.

Primary school responses

Since the publication of the HMI primary survey in 1978, a sector of education which had largely been taken for granted since the Plowden Report eleven years earlier has been the scene of considerable activity. Primary classrooms have become popular settings for researchers; inspectors and advisers have run courses and produced guideline booklets; and in the schools themselves, teachers have begun to reflect critically and collectively on their curriculum programmes.

It would, though, be wrong to suppose the HMI survey to be the sole cause of this activity. The concern with school accountability which finally took formal shape in Mr Callaghan's Ruskin speech of 1976 had already influenced the attitudes of parents and teachers, so that the survey findings landed on prepared and broadly sympathetic ears. Teachers' organisations seized on the survey's favourable report on the teaching of basics as a vindication of current practice. But teachers themselves took a more realistic view and the survey's sharp comments on neglected knowledge areas, the need for whole curriculum planning and better matching of work to pupil ability have been taken seriously. Following the survey, national and local publications have given a further stimulus to the extent that an altogether more critical, self-questioning climate can be found in many primary schools compared with the cosy assumptions of the 1960s and early 1970s.

151

All this is to be welcomed. Less welcome have been the effects of falling rolls, which have already emptied some primary schools and depleted the range of staff expertise in others. And as always, the accountability movement has generated a climate of cutbacks in educational spending which has been intensified under the 1979 Thatcher administration. Perhaps the only incidental benefit from falling rolls has been the movement to save small rural primary schools by fostering curriculum links between them. Given the rather insular, self-contained thinking which often seemed a characteristic of the 1960s primary school, this new trend marks a major shift of opinion from which many secondary schools are still exempt. It is now clear that a rise in the birthrate will lead to some expansion in primary schools – at least in some areas – in the late 1980s. If this expansion is based on inter-school co-operation rather than individual school concerns, resources are likely to be better used and what had been forced on the schools as a necessity will become of positive educational advantage. The second case study shows how such co-operation has been of real value.

The revival of curriculum development in primary schools has not been unnoticed by commercial interests, and the HMI advocacy of resource-based subjects like science has caused shoals of leaflets to fall on headteachers' desks. In some cases, the temptation to purchase books and equipment of doubtful value may have impoverished other curriculum activities. Certainly heads and teachers in primary schools find themselves sharing decisions and making judgments more vigorously and extensively than in previous years, when – ironically – curriculum funding was easier to come by.

It is not possible to give a detailed view of this activity, neither is the secondary school device of displaying the curriculum structure of much value in examining the work of a primary school. And a case study of a primary school would need to be a substantial affair, looking closely not only at the shared intentions of head and staff but also at the fine grain of life in its classrooms. This would fall outside the remit of this book.

Instead, I offer some notes on the kinds of strategies and approaches to curriculum planning which have arisen in two primary schools. Both happen to be in the same local area, but they operate in quite different local contexts. Yet the similarities in their view of curriculum activity are perhaps more striking than the differences. Extracts are given of working papers produced at the schools in the belief that while this account of school responses makes no pretence to be representative, it will none the less be helpful to schools involved in curriculum development and also illustrate a continuity of style in tackling curriculum problems which has already been noted in considering change in secondary schools.

1 Bassett's Farm School, Exmouth, Devon

This new open-plan 5–11 primary school opened in 1978 as a result of private and council estate building on the outskirts of Exmouth, a seaside town in east Devon. The head (Mrs Jean Halton) had taught in the area for some years, and the school intake shows a wide social mix. She and her staff were able to work closely with the county architect when the second phase of the school was built and take advantage of their experience with the original open-plan building.

There are 220 pupils and eight staff, including the head who teaches every day from 10.15 a.m. onwards, except for one uninterrupted morning for administration and planning. There are frequent lunchtime staff meetings, and a regular pattern of after school planning meetings. There is a deputy head, and two staff have scale 2 posts. These three serve as team leaders for the curriculum in the upper junior school, lower junior school and infant school respectively. Their main priority is the day-to-day management of these teams; next, liaison with other teams; and lastly, staff development by recognising and encouraging particular talents among staff.

A single large comprehensive school – Exmouth School – offers 11–18 education for pupils in a large area around Exmouth. The heads of the secondary and primary schools constitute an 'academic council' for the Exmouth area, and this has promoted not only close co-operation between the comprehensive school and its contributory schools, but also curriculum initiatives among the primary schools in collaboration with secondary school staff. Working parties have devised an agreed common programme for language, published a document on study skills, and a document on the teaching of history and geography in primary schools is in preparation. The county advisory service has also produced helpful curriculum guides.

Just as in a good comprehensive school, the visitor to Bassett's Farm School is struck by the atmosphere of purposeful informality, of unseen yet firm control, of intentional structure within a format of individual and group work. Teachers have an alertness, a quickness of response which seems to be missing from formal classrooms and rows of desks: pupil behaviour is relaxed yet orderly, the staff constantly stimulating learning and responding to pupils in ways which make nonsense of the idea that the personal development of pupils can in some way be separated from their academic programme. The single activity is education and it is a whole, entire process.

None of this happens by chance. As always, the true art is to conceal art; the seeming ease and smoothness with which the arts of curriculum planning have been applied conceal sustained thinking and a reflective approach which underpins and informs practice. The following remarks of the head, jotted down during our conversation and now put together, will give some idea of what is involved:

'The effect of the HMI survey, and other reports, has been to make you think about what you're doing. Teachers, for instance, are looking at study skills with far more accuracy. We want pupils to observe closely, and to some extent this runs counter to a society where people watch rather than do, listen rather than read. It's a matter of redressing the balance – pupils may not be accustomed to this at home. For us teachers, too, it means a shift of attitude, an eye for critical detail.

'We've talked a lot about the problems of primary science, about organising small groups of pupils. Some heads thought the primary survey placed too much stress on physical science. We're trying to make science a part of curriculum work: for example, our "Houses and Homes" project links science with history and geography. There are a host of books on study skills, and this can lead to contrived situations. But by careful planning you can arrange for them to arise naturally.

'In an open-plan school teachers must be structured. Since we were a new school, we took the opportunity to think the curriculum through together. We have after school clubs for pupils every evening, but we can arrange to meet in staff groups from 3 to 6 p.m. and plan co-operative teaching.

'The human element is of enormous importance – it's all about human beings working together. I've got staff who were trained in the 1960s, when colleges put more stress on personal relationships in classrooms than on skills. I think this is why they can diagnose pupil needs very quickly. There are dangers in putting too much stress on skill acquisition: the arts of class teaching are what matter and I'm worried that tomorrow's teachers might not have them at their fingertips.

'Structuring means careful records: teachers adapt work to match the child's own abilities, and a detailed record is kept of mathematics and language skills. I encourage staff to make these honest impressions of each pupil's work every six months, and they are open for parents to see for themselves at any time.

'We approach history and geography through thematic work. This needs care: a teacher can get stuck in a groove while pursuing a theme, but on the other hand you cannot be too prescriptive. Infant work, in particular, must be more spontaneous: we aim to encourage independent learning and show them how to take care of themselves. This calls for careful judgments. We hope to give our pupils a sense of history, a sense of scientific inquiry. It is not so much a matter of elaborate apparatus, more of fostering observation by asking the right questions.

'There is a place for tests – we use them to diagnose weaknesses in punctuation, spelling, mathematics concepts, map reading and so on. But they can easily be overdone. We don't use commercial spelling tests: getting pupils to write down a dictated passage may be old-fashioned, but it tests listening skills and concentration as well as spelling. The closer assessment is to the curriculum work of the teacher, the better. Some of the assessment devices one reads about seem so clinical and remote – compiling grids on qualities like curiosity and observation, and so on. Tests should be diagnostic and come out of the teaching.'

In addition to a parents' handbook, the school has produced an extensive list of documents for staff use. There are policy statements for mathematics, language, health education and physical education, guidelines for music and science, and general guidelines for staff. There are further statements on proposals for integrated project work, and clearly the staff have developed the art of working together so as to devise effective learning experiences. Written statements alone cannot guarantee such experiences: but they can clear up uncertainties and give useful pointers once the right climate has been established.

The following extract from a paper produced by the head in autumn 1981, after staff discussion, will indicate the kind of considerations which staff take into account:

Bassett's Farm County Primary School

PROJECTS: GENERAL COMMENTS

The main way of teaching history, geography and environmental studies will be through integration of these subjects into a main theme, also incorporating as many other aspects as possible (mathematics, English, religious education, music, drama, art and craft). It is, therefore, important that the choice of projects should be carefully made and then planned to meet the requirements of the different age groups.

Enthusiasm and stimulation are the two most important factors and children should be encouraged to develop their own interests within the overall project.

Planning the project

It is worth asking yourself some leading questions before starting the project:

1 Will each child cover all the ground, or will various groups cover different aspects and report back?
2 How shall I devise and set tasks for the children to complete?
3 How will the children be grouped?
4 How can I make best use of the skills of the teachers involved?
5 How will the information and material be recorded and presented?
6 To what extent will the contributory subjects be integrated?
7 What areas of knowledge and understanding will be covered?

The best way to instigate a project is through the teacher who is the most valuable resource in the school. It is the teachers who will maintain the standard and by their enthusiasm ensure its success.

Use a flow chart to indicate ground to be covered. Explore *all* the possibilities, even if you decide only to develop some of them. Integration should be as natural as possible and not contrived to include every subject. It should be flexible enough to include spontaneous ideas but at the same time retain its original purpose.

156

METHOD

How do we involve the children?

1 The topic must be introduced in such a way that the child is immediately stimulated. Therefore, it is a good idea to start with:

(a) a visit
(b) a film/slide show
(c) a visiting speaker
(d) a sound track

2 The class/group is then divided into groups to develop their own areas by means of lessons and follow-up work. If the whole year group is working together the teachers have to decide on their own topic areas and prepare lessons and materials for the group they are going to teach. A high degree of guidance is necessary to encourage enthusiasm. It is an *absolute waste of time* to put a pile of books on the table and expect children to develop their own areas of study – all they do is copy off great chunks – just as when they had a formal writing lesson.

3 We must ensure that:

(a) books are pre-selected and of the right reading level
(b) relevant sections are indicated or that older children know how to look them up
(c) sufficient guidance is given on:
      How to use the books
      How to re-present the materials
      Standard of work required

The earlier stages of a project benefit from work sheets produced by the teacher which contain information, questions, instructions and reference notes. (The children do not write on these sheets – only use them as guidance.) The work sheets should also contain suggestions for further areas of study –which will encourage the children to explore the associated aspects.

ACTIVITIES

1 These are almost too numerous to mention; nevertheless . . . children will write stories, poems, accounts, news items and notes. They will make verbal reports and descriptions to each other and on tape. They will draw and paint, make models and generally explore all the art media along with taking

photographs and dramatising the situation. The possibilities are endless and every child should be encouraged to explore as many avenues as possible, thereby expanding their own interests.

2 Written work can be kept in folders, topic books or exercise books. The drawings, maps etc. on plain paper and the writing on lined paper. It can then be mounted if needed for the display. We think standards are very important and all work should be carefully presented and frequently changed.

3 *Displays*

The best displays are arrived at by everyone involved discussing them.
Topic – What's available – position of display – How shall we mount it? – Audience!
At the beginning of the project the display area probably contains books/pictures/natural objects, A.V.A. etc. that will stimulate the children.
This should gradually change to a final display which will be on exhibition of all the work produced by the children, hopefully to a high standard.

4 *Evaluation*

This is most important and at the end of each project an evaluation should be written in your record book. What did the children get out of it? What was unsuccessful? Have the children developed new skills and attitudes? Have their imaginations been extended? etc., etc.
Obviously, all the teachers involved will have been discussing the project as they have gone along, but it is important as a group to ask these questions. Have the children:

(a) enjoyed the project and become more aware of their environment?
(b) remembered basic information?
(c) developed their powers of observation?
(d) learnt to use books for reference?
(e) been able to record their findings?
(f) been extended enough?
(g) written and presented their work attractively?

Sub-grouping

Not all children can keep pace with the majority of the class. They can, however, make a valuable contribution if they are given a little extra help. Here are a few suggestions:

1 Simpler work sheets – could be written on or coloured
2 Smaller work load
3 Directions towards pictures or models
4 Use of cassette recorder for reporting facts or telling stories
    – very valuable for the child who cannot read or write fluently but who is stimulated by visual materials.

RESOURCES

The school has the following equipment:
2 colour televisions
5 radio cassette recorders
6 cassette players
3 language masters
3 junction boxes and 18 headphones
4 slide viewers
2 cameras – 1 instamatic, 1 polaroid
1 film strip slide projector
1 overhead projector
1 heat copier
1 Banda machine
1 Roneo duplicator
1 jumbo typewriter
1 video cassette recorder.

2 Woodbury Primary School, Devon

This Church of England primary school was built in 1872 in the centre of an east Devon village, which currently has about two thousand inhabitants and a new housing estate under construction. The original buildings have been modernised and a new wing was added to the school in 1960. Facilities include a new school library, a science and practical working bay, an environmental studies and garden area, a language laboratory and a refurbished open-air swimming pool. These have been added as a result of co-operation between the local authority and parents.

There are at present 45 children on roll aged from four to eleven and 2.2 staff (two full-time) in addition to the head (Graham Rowland). The staff have produced a detailed document *Curriculum Planning and Development at Woodbury Primary School* to assist their own development, and for the information of governors, the LEA and other visitors. This is a substantial publication which combines summaries of relevant documents with statements of curriculum policy and practice. Thus there are helpful extracts from DES curriculum documents; from Schools Council publications on the whole curriculum, environmental studies and moral education; and from the HMI primary survey, the Bullock report on language and the HMI booklet on mathematics 5–11. The document covers all areas of the curriculum and illuminates school policy with examples of actual programmes.

The Devon LEA as a matter of policy sponsors its Co-operation of Small Schools (COSS) project, and this school is a member of such a project along with two neighbouring schools. Early in 1981, after some preliminary soundings, the three heads met to establish the project and its results so far have been most encouraging.

The head of the school devotes 80 per cent of his time to teaching, with responsibility for the upper juniors. The following extract from my conversation with the head will illustrate the school's approach to the curriculum:

'From the head's point of view, the HMI primary survey offers a useful overall view of the curriculum. The schedules in its appendix of factors which influenced HMI judgment can guide us too: we don't have to waste time rediscovering the wheel. Some have interpreted the HMI survey as advocating a return to basics. This is unjust, but the survey does provide useful checkpoints for action and guidance to set alongside the more "romantic" view evident in the Plowden Report.

'There are no scaled posts here, so it's important to develop the professionalism of staff through the curriculum. We have no "specialist" teachers, and so we try to make use of LEA advice from advisers and advisory teachers. We each try to acquire a specialist skill – one of my staff has done this for science – and we interchange among ourselves so as to give all pupils the benefit. The COSS linkage scheme between our three rural primary schools does this, too.

'We retain the traditional focus on the teacher in her class as the pastoral agent and link in curriculum planning. He or she knows what is realistic with his or her children. Everything is interpreted at classroom level. The temptation must be resisted to run a "polyfilla" curriculum: for example, to look for a gap into which science can be plugged. It would be unfortunate if the primary survey's observations on science teaching were to be interpreted in that way, with say, one hour a week for science as a separate subject. Planning by parts is frustrating.

'We aim to look at the curriculum as a whole, and to see science as another way of exploiting critical thinking. Our COSS project "Watermark", which the three schools have devised together, aims to offer experiences in science as part of an integrated studies scheme. We want teachers to see the environment as a resource for learning.

'I think teachers enjoy giving an account of what they are doing. Our aim is to clarify our thinking, to look for continuity and progression in our work, to reflect on what we do and ask ourselves: "how does this match what we want to achieve?" At the same time, we see the importance in the classroom of the teacher's ready and intuitive response.'

The school is a member of the academic council for the Exmouth area, and makes use of the study skills documents which have been prepared within the council. At 3.30 p.m. every day, the staff of the school meet for discussion and planning.

Two extracts follow which throw further light on the work of this school. The first shows the curriculum plan for part of the humanities curriculum, and an example of the pupil materials prepared for the COSS 'Watermark' project. The second draws upon the COSS 'Joint curriculum evaluation paper' – prepared after the first year of the COSS scheme – to illustrate the considerations which have influenced the scheme:

(i) Curriculum Materials

Extract from 'Clean water', COSS 'Watermark' Project:

A   Discuss with your partner(s).

Before people had taps and piped water where did they get their water to drink? Make a list like the one below.

SOURCES OF WATER IN THE OLDEN DAYS (Copy and complete.)

1 ....

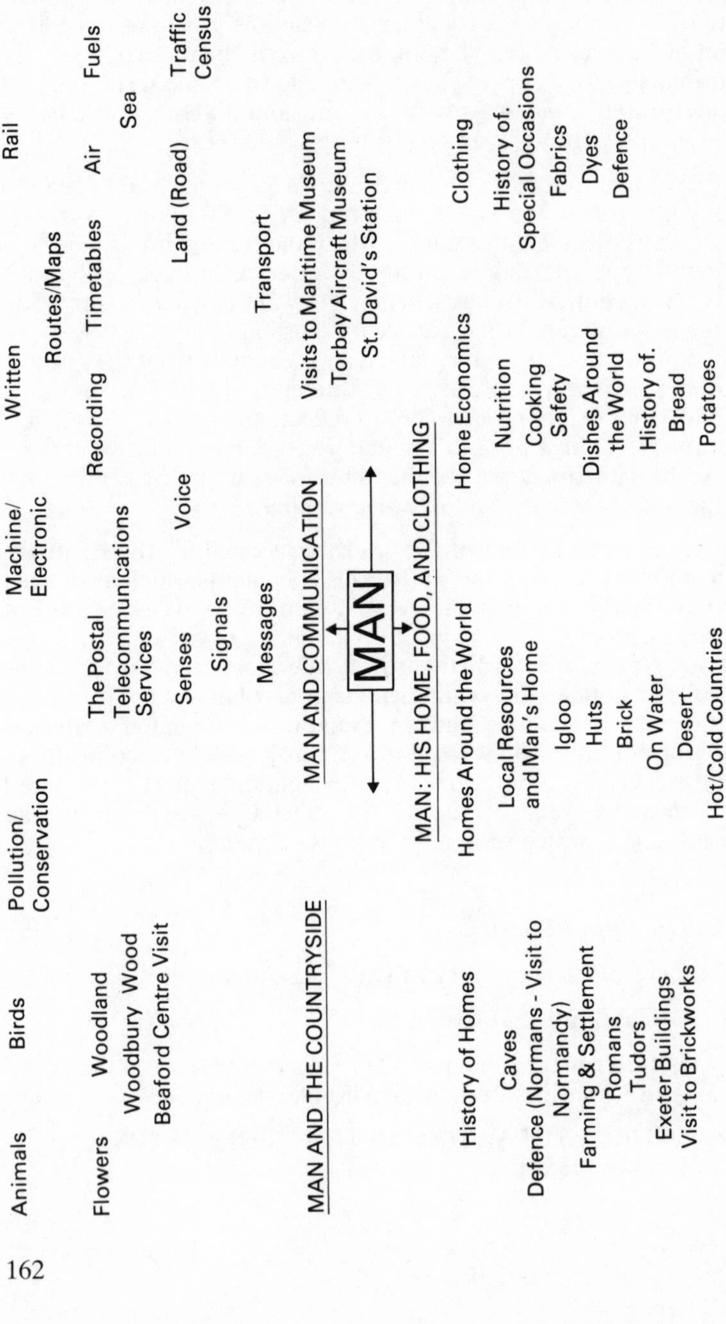

Animals   Birds   Pollution/   Written   Rail

Flowers   Woodland   Conservation

Woodbury Wood

Beaford Centre Visit

Machine/   Recording   Timetables   Air   Fuels

Electronic   Routes/Maps   Sea

The Postal   Land (Road)   Traffic Census

Telecommunications

Services   Voice

Senses   Transport

Signals

Messages   Visits to Maritime Museum

Torbay Aircraft Museum

St. David's Station

MAN AND THE COUNTRYSIDE

MAN AND COMMUNICATION

MAN

MAN: HIS HOME, FOOD, AND CLOTHING

Homes Around the World   Home Economics   Clothing

Local Resources   Nutrition   History of.

and Man's Home   Cooking   Special Occasions

Igloo   Safety   Fabrics

Huts   Dishes Around   Dyes

Brick   the World   Defence

On Water   History of.

Desert   Bread

Hot/Cold Countries   Potatoes

History of Homes

Caves

Defence (Normans - Visit to

Normandy)

Farming & Settlement

Romans

Tudors

Exeter Buildings

Visit to Brickworks

Figure 3.10 Extract from humanities curriculum: environmental

2 ....

3 ....

4 ....

5 ....

6 ....

7 ....

8 ....

B   Are there any signs of these water sources near where you live? Discuss with your partners and make a list.

C   Rainwater which collects in reservoirs or underground is *NOT* clean enough to drink. It has many small bits or particles in it ALGAE (plants) PROTOZOA (small animals) BACTERIA (germs). The water is often muddy and would have an unpleasant taste. Even worse very dangerous diseases, such as TYPHOID and CHOLERA are carried in infected water.

D   Write briefly and draw a diagram about unclean water.

Today our water passes through a waterworks where bits are *FILTERED* out and a special chemical CHLORINE kills the germs.

Discuss with your partner and record your answers with diagrams.

Why is clean water important?

Where else at school might you smell Chlorine?

Chlorine is used to make household cleaners such as – VIM, DOMESTOS, and DOT. Why?

Prepare a short talk or play about the dangers of unclean water.
*WARNING: CHLORINE IS VERY DANGEROUS

(ii) COSS Scheme

Extract from 'Co-operation of Small Schools Project: a Joint Curriculum Evaluation Paper, 1982':

In this instance the schools which were willing to actively

explore extensive co-operative possibilities were those

   (i)   with between 35 – 55 children on roll
  (ii)   which had Head + 1.1 or Head + 2.2 teachers
 (iii)   which had Headteachers who admitted some curriculum deficiencies as well as particular strengths in their schools
 (iv)   which were committed to the idea of reciprocity
  (v)   where the Headteachers had good interpersonal relations
 (vi)   where the Headteachers felt they could "sell" the idea to their respective staffs
(vii)   which were within 30 minutes travelling distance of each other.

A Way Forward

Early in 1981 the Headmasters of the three small primary schools at Aylesbeare, Woodbury and Woodbury Salterton met together to plan positive steps forward in co-operation. A member of the L.E.A. advisory staff was to be present but owing to illness was unable to be present and was kept informed by correspondence.

From the outset the Heads established that the project would be conducted in a voluntary spirit, that ideas and reservations could be frankly discussed, differences of opinions would be respected, and that the speed of the project would be determined by mutual agreement.

A wide ranging discussion of the curriculum facilities and staff enthusiasms and weaknesses of the various schools took place and in the voluntary spirit of 'we could offer to the C.O.S.S. project ...' it was quickly established that particular needs might be met by sharing resources and teachers: One school had a large hall, another a pottery studio, and teachers in the various schools could offer curriculum leadership in science, environmental studies, pottery, and health education.

It was then agreed that the Headteachers should fully consult their respective staffs as to their views (informal discussions had been undertaken during the early tentative phases) and to explore practical teaching and transport arrangements.

Following staff meetings within each school and a further Headteachers' meeting a combined meeting of all the teaching staff of the three schools was held at which the proposal was made that the junior children from these schools should join together on Wednesdays throughout the term and that the children would spend three Wednesdays at each school where they would participate in the following courses:

Aylesbeare   :   Environmental studies

Woodbury   :   Science and health education

Wood/Salterton :   Pottery and craft

The last hour of each Wednesday was to be reserved for combined games.

At a meeting between the Headteachers and a representative of the L.E.A. advisory staff both transport and some financial assistance were agreed. Permission and support from parents and governors was sought and obtained.

Joint 'Watermark' Project:

Overall Objectives

To provide a foundation Science Course entitled "Water":
Floating, Sinking, Density for the top juniors of the three schools.

To give a range of practical experiences in pottery slab/tiles/coil/thumb pots.

To explore the work of the R.N.L.I. rescue and survival in Water.

To examine in a Health Education context the Water Cycle, Clean and Polluted Water, Body and Hygiene Needs for Water.

Organisation

(a)   A maximum of 9 hours were spent on the Science Water Scheme with 3 weeks of 3 hour sessions. Children working in groups of 8 with a teacher of student. Scheme used 'Nuffield Combined Science'.

(b)   Pottery 4 hours Groups of 10

(c)   Health Education 4 hours Groups of 10 – 15

(d)   Environmental Studies 6 hours Groups of 10

(e)   Games, although programmed for 9 hours only 3 took place (See below).

Assessment

Assessments of levels of pupils' performance were made by the children's own school teacher. Much consultation between teachers as to assignments set, style of handwriting, levels of expectation took place.

A slide photographic record of the children and their work was undertaken throughout.

Reactions to the COSS Project:

Although no one in the scheme would claim everything has been perfect the reactions from children and staff have been extremely positive and encouraging as is suggested by the "Additional Co-operations" already undertaken.

The children have thoroughly enjoyed their 'visits' to the other schools, enjoyed being hosts at their own schools, and benefited widely in the social and academic spheres. Their reaction and close consultation has brought wide support from parents and governors.

The support given by the teaching staffs (whose ages range from 23 to 60) has made a whole new venture not only work but an enjoyable, professionally stimulating experience which it is planned to continue throughout 1982.

The most frequent criticism by staff of the project has been 'not enough time'. Ideas have abounded and expectations, in a positive atmosphere, high. When the Science, Pottery and Environmental Studies programmes have been progressing well there has been a reluctance to 'break off' for Games – thus only 3 of the 9 planned hours of combined games have taken place in the Autumn term. These factors will need careful balancing in the next term.

The attitudes of staff are more positive towards the 'other' schools although some remnant of 'they need us more than we need them' may on some occasions remain: the autonomous traditions of schools will take more than one year to vanish!

Differences in teaching styles, classroom organisation etc. have not hindered the project. Rather the recognition of steps forward, however small, has been encouraged.

In contrast to the Head who declared that he '... could not find the time for all the work involved in co-operation schemes ...' the Heads involved in this C.O.S.S. project have found an easing of some of the workload: i.e. in sharing it with professional colleagues. In place of the attempt by one teacher to provide Science *and* Pottery *and* Health Education *and* Environmental Studies for the children, a TEAM approach has brought specialism, enthusiasm, leadership and provision for a larger number of children.

Resumé of Critical Points

(a)   Promotion of good interpersonal relations/trust

(b) Frequent and positive communication
(c) Sensitive 'sounding out' of others – negotiating a voluntary agreement
(d) Recognition of weaknesses in one's own school/teaching
(e) Commitment to reciprocity : Genuine co-operation and sharing
(f) Full consultation with L.E.A./Staff/Ancillary staff (i.e. School meals service, secretaries)/Parents/Governors, prior to and during the project
(g) Recognition of efforts by staff
(h) Encouragement and support of TEAM approach
(i) Sharing of equipment, joint purchases, and joint financial planning and
(j) A sense of humour when things go wrong!

Final note

Two specific points relating to this interesting and productive exercise in primary school co-operation may be of interest. First, the LEA has so far met the travel costs of pupils during this initial phase of the scheme. Second, there has been scarcely any evidence of school chauvinism: none of the schools' parent-teacher associations, for instance, has objected to the use of purchased equipment by pupils from other schools.

Appendix A
Abbreviations and subject codes

A	art		De	design
AEB	Associated Examining Board for GCE		DFL	design for living
			Dr	drama
Am	American studies			
As	assembly		E	English language/lit.
			Ea	expressive arts
B	biology		Ec	economics
Bd	building		Eu	European studies
Bg	British government, constitution		Ev	environmental science/studies
Bi	British industrial society		Ex	electronics
C	chemistry		F	French
Ca	careers education		Fm	film studies
CA	creative activities/arts/studies		Fp	form period
Cd	child development, child studies		G	geography
CDT	craft, design and technology		Ga	organised games
			Gc	graphics
Ci	citizenship		GCE	General Certificate of Education
Cm	communication		Ge	geology
Co	commerce		Gk	classical Greek
Cp	computer studies		Gm	German
Cr	crafts		Gs	general studies
Cs	classical studies			
CSE	Certificate of Secondary Education		H	history
			Hb	human biology
Ct	control technology		He	health education
Cy	community education/ studies/service		Hk	home economics
			Hu	humanities

I	Italian	R	Russian
Is	integrated studies	Re	religious education
		RLDU	Resources for Learning Development Unit (Bristol)
Je	jewelry		
JMB	Joint Matriculation Board for GCE	Rm	remedial provision
		Rs	rural studies/science
L	Latin		
La	foreign languages		
Li	library		
Ls	leisure studies	S	science, general science, integrated science
M	mathematics	SCISP	Schools Council Integrated Science Project
MAT	mixed ability teaching		
Me	moral education		
Mk	metalwork	Se	social education
Mu	music	Sh	shorthand
Mv	motor vehicle studies	SMP	Schools Mathematics Project
Nk	needlework, fabric craft	So	sociology, social studies
		Sp	Spanish
O	office practice		
P	physics		
Pa	physical activities	T	typing
Pc	physics with chemistry	Td	technical and engineering drawing
Pe	physical education (can include Ga)		
		Tk	technology
Pg	political education, politics, government	Tp	tutor period
		Tr	traffic education
Ph	photography	Tv	television studies
Po	pottery		
Ps	private study		
PSM	Personal, social and moral education/development	Wk	woodwork
		Ws	world studies

Appendix B   Curriculum notation

Chapter 2 ends with the simulation study *Brobdingnag School*, and the notation used to display its curriculum structure is used also for the case studies in Chapter 3. This notation originated in 1969 before the notion of the common curriculum was widespread, and was devised to display the intricate setting, streaming and option schemes associated with the traditional core-plus-option curriculum. It is much less satisfactory for displaying common curriculum structures. However, it has been taken up by HMI and subsequently popularised, and is at least a widely understood notation for summarising curriculums. Its use is therefore recommended. More detailed accounts of this notation will be found in Eustace and Wilcox (1977) and ILEA (1979).

The Brobdingnag simulation will be used to illustrate how the notation works (Figure AB.1).

1P	30	M_6 E_6 G_2 H_2	Ga	S_4 F_4	$\left[\begin{smallmatrix}Wk\\Hk\end{smallmatrix}\right]_2$	$\left[\begin{smallmatrix}Mk\\Nk\end{smallmatrix}\right]_2$	A_2 Re_2 Mu_2 Pe_2 Dr_2
1W	31	" " " "	Ga	" "	" "	" "	" " " " "
1R	31	" " " "	Ga	" "	" "	" "	" " " " "
1E	30	" " " "	Ga	" "	" "	" "	" " " " "
1S	28	M_8 Is_{12}	Ga	S_2 Rs_4	Wk	A_2	Mu_2 Pe Dr_2
1C	28	" "	Ga	" "	Mk ▼	"	" Pe "
1H	27	" " + Rm$_{16}$	Ga$_2$	" "	Hk / Nk$_4$	"	" Pe$_2$ "

The dotted lines separating the four forms 1PWRE show that these each contain pupils of all abilities. But the solid line separating 1PWRE from 1SCH shows that there is differentiation by ability, and that the first year pupils are arranged in two broad ability bands.

1P	30
1W	31
1R	31
1E	30
1S	28
1C	28
1H	27

This notation would indicate that the pupils were placed in seven separate streamed forms.

1P	30
1W	31
1R	31
1E	30
1S	28
1C	28
1H	27

This shows that the two bands are not split by ability, but are two parallel populations (to facilitate timetabling).

This is evidently a 7 fe (seven forms of entry) school.

Figure AB.1

The top line shows that – reading from left to right – form 1P has six periods of mathematics, six of English, two of geography and so on. (See Appendix A for list of subject codes.) The repeat marks show that the other forms in this band – 1WRE – are getting the same programme. Similarly, in the lower band pupils get eight periods of mathematics, twelve of integrated studies (which evidently consists of E, G, H and Re, since these subjects are not otherwise listed), two of science and so on. The lower bracket (Figure AB.2) indicates that sixteen additional periods of remedial help are offered within this band for both mathematics and English. We cannot determine how the sixteen periods are split between the two.

171

Figure AB.2

Figure AB.3

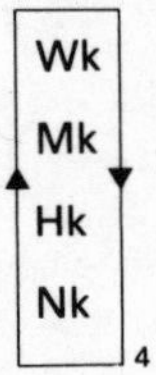

Figure AB.4

The 'block' around woodwork and home economics for 1P (Figure AB.3) shows that both Wk and Hk are *simultaneously offered* to these pupils for two periods, and that the distribution of pupils between the two subjects is *not according to ability*. We can assume that in this case it is according to gender, the boys doing Wk and the girls Hk. The same applies to the two periods blocked out for Mk and Nk, and this arrangement repeats, form by form, for each of the four forms in this band. It will be noted that this results in sets of less than twenty in each of these technical subjects.

The same subjects are offered in a more economical and non-divisive way in the lower band. As before, the block (Figure AB.4) shows that the four subjects are timetabled together. But the arrows show that some *rotation system* operates, to ensure that for at least part of the year, each pupil samples each of the four subjects. We can assume that the 73 pupils in this band are split into four mixed groups of boys and girls, each of about eighteen pupils. This uses staff more effectively and avoids the gender split, but each pupil will spend less time on any given subject in the block. Evidently this arrangement must reflect some different educational principle from that used in the top band, as well as leading to a saving of staff.

Whereas Pe is taught by forms – both sexes together, evidently, with one teacher – in the top band, in the lower band it is blocked into four groups. We can assume there are two parallel groups each for boys and girls. The only subject which cuts across the ability line is games: here, the entire first year of 195 pupils is divided between eight staff, presumably so that a range of games and activities can be provided.

The Brobdingnag second year follows similar lines, but for the top band both mathematics and French are arranged into four groups by ability, for five and four periods respectively. The open bracket (Figure AB.5) indicates that the groups are *simultaneously timetabled* and *grouped by ability or attainment*. Similarly, there is *setting* in English for the lower band in year 2.

M

M

M

M
5

Figure AB.5

Figure AB.6

B	C	P
B	C	P
B	C	P
B_2	C_2	P_2

Figure AB.7

In the upper band, there is simultaneous blocking (Figure AB.6) of Latin and German into four groups, not by ability. This is evidently an *option pool*, with pupils free to choose one or other foreign language. (It is possible that pupils are allocated to these groups. The notation does not rule out this possibility, but it is unlikely.)

In year 3, the only new notation is for the three science subjects (Figure AB.7). This shows that the same setting by ability is applied to all of them: the scientists have agreed on identical sets.

In years 4 and 5, the dotted line marks a division between core and options. In the core, CA options and the DFL course, along with games as before, span the entire year group. The options are arranged into two bands, with an extra option pool in the upper band and a lower time allocation per pool.

From the point of view of the common curriculum, the grouping of pupils and the organisation of the work within blocks is of especial significance. The examples in Figure AB.8 illustrate some important configurations.

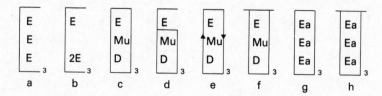

Figure AB.8

a   Three ability sets for English.
b   One top set, and two lower parallel sets.
c   An option between English, music and drama for all pupils.
d   One top set for English, and the rest of the pupils opt for music or drama.
e   Pupils rotate between E, Mu and D, experiencing each in three non-ability groups.
f   E, Mu and D are team taught for all pupils. They are not discrete elements, as in e, but are coherently organised in such a way that their separate identity is retained.
g   E, Mu and D have been integrated into Ea. Greater coherence means they forfeit their separate subject identities. But the three groups function separate from each other.
h   As for g; but the three groups are operating as a team.

Notes

1 Problems and prescriptions – the curriculum context

1 This approach to curriculum development is summarised from the full and enormously useful account given in W. Reid (1978).
2 This treatment, too, is taken from W. Reid (1981a), who sees it as an interpretation of arguments originally set out by Schwab (1969).
3 For a further and particularly helpful discussion of theory and practice in institutional contexts, see Golby (1981).
4 A useful account of these issues will be found in Golby and Lawton (1981). It should be noted that there is much theoretical writing on the curriculum, and W. Reid (1981b) offers a helpful categorisation of contributors based on two considerations: first, how people relate to the actual world of schools, and second, on the extent to which they approach the curriculum in an exploratory way or, by contrast, with some set of overarching principles in mind. Thus *systemic* writers accept schools and work with them, but seek to change them by applying predetermined views on control and planning (this corresponds to what I have here termed the procedural or technocratic approach); *radicals* apply their ideals to schools not as they are, but as they might be (much sociological writing falls into this category); *existentialists* concentrate on individual growth, free of institutions or general principles; while the *deliberative* approach works in the context of social institutions but approaches problems without *a priori* preconceptions or principles. The latter approach is favoured here.

Thus, for example, Hargreaves (1982), writing about the comprehensive school, proposes that its curriculum should have a central core 'for pupils between the ages of eleven and fourteen or fifteen, which should be organised around community studies and the expressive arts'. He rejects the radical perspective, which sees schooling as it exists as unacceptable, and recognises that schools must be changed from what they are by some set of transactions. But he derives his curriculum ideals from the sociological theories of Durkheim and others, and therefore lies in the systemic camp. His book is an interesting exploration of the slippery concept of community education, but lies outside the deliberative perspective which sees curriculum problems as yielding not to formal precepts but to moral decisions between committed individuals in particular institutions.

5 The Schools Council funded the Keele Integrated Studies Project from 1968 to 1974. Its published materials bring together work in English, history and geography for pupils aged eleven to thirteen.

6 A discussion of the Yellow Book and associated curriculum developments in the DES will be found in Lawton (1980).

7 For a penetrating study of the 'great debate' and its futility, see W. Reid (1978).

8 There is an interesting discussion of DES, HMI and core curriculum issues in Golby (1980).

9 The covert ways of the DES were heavily criticised by a visiting team of distinguished OECD officials (OECD, 1976). They concluded that the DES had, by virtue of the privileged position afforded civil servants in Britain, become 'a power in its own right', and that this power was buttressed by the confidentiality enshrined in the Official Secrets Act and civil service tradition: 'The preservation of this powerful position, by combining the task of coherent planning with defensive tactics, excluding an open planning process, public hearings or, even, participation, seems to an outside observer as a mixture of strength and weakness.'

10 In 1969 the Schools Council organised a conference on the secondary curriculum at Scarborough. In the account of this conference (Schools Council, 1971), there occurs this passage:

> Is there a need to look at the whole conception of secondary education? . . . One group, in defining the curriculum, was moving towards considerations of this kind, while an HMI representative pointed out that there was a group in the Inspectorate already giving it serious thought. He defined the essentials of a good curriculum as giving importance to personal development, aesthetic experience, experience of the material world and of society, and 'transcendentalism' – ideals and inspiration.

It seems clear – from this rare glimpse of the HMI at work – that the basic structure of what was to become the 'eight areas of experience' (DES, 1977a) already existed within the Inspectorate in the late 1960s.

11 The work of the APU is examined in some detail in Holt (1981).

12 The argument that pupils have a *right* to a core curriculum is a philosophical one, originally presented in White (1973).

13 The suggestion that education has a cultural basis was developed by Raymond Williams in *The Long Revolution* (1961). It was elaborated as the basis for a common curriculum in Lawton (1973).

14 The defects of option schemes in years 4 and 5 are revealed very

clearly in a school-based study by Hurman (1978).

15 For a measured and effective attack on the objectives model of curriculum development, see Stenhouse (1975).

16 Consideration of wider issues in selecting from the culture is given in Skilbeck and Reynolds (1976).

17 Hirst (1965) is a seminal paper which has had much influence on thinking *about* curriculum planning, but much less on the practice of curriculum in schools. Hirst put his ideas into lively and direct form in a brief article (Schools Council, 1967) but it had little effect. Hirst suggested that different forms of knowledge could be identified by determining differences in the logical structure of their central concepts. It has been argued that this takes too narrow a view of cultural experience: see, for example, the critique in Skilbeck (1976). Even so, Hirst's attempt to guide the business of selecting from the culture challenges the narrowness of the conventional grammar school curriculum with its neglect of performance subjects, and can help a school take a view of the whole curriculum (Holt, 1978).

Hirst, for example, makes it clear that *religion* counts as a 'distinct discipline or form of knowledge' (Hirst, 1965). But the HMI, in *Curriculum 11–16*, list 'the spiritual' as one of their eight areas of experience, and link it exclusively with 'a sense of God or of Gods. Spiritual is a meaningless adjective for the atheist . . . '. But it can be argued that this is to confuse the religious and the spiritual: 'Spirituality (is) a much wider concept which would include religious belief but could not be tied down to it' (Neal, 1982). Generalised terms to describe parts of a map of the culture are of little value in curriculum building if we do not know how they have been arrived at.

18 More recently, Hirst has written that 'In the sixties . . . the search for fundamental categories and principles was thought to be somewhat easier than has proved to be the case. . . . My own [work] on forms of knowledge [is a clear example] of premature confidence in this respect' (Hirst, 1982). The difficulty is only partly a matter of analysing concepts and thus marking out distinctive knowledge areas: it is also a question of beliefs about the nature of knowledge and moral values: of what view one is to take of the nature of liberal education. W. Reid (1980) argues that Hirst 'reduces liberal education to a positivist, intellectual education in which truth is conceived as being empirically demonstrable', and suggests instead that liberal education is 'as Schwab and the authors of the Harvard Report prefer to believe, the management of an inherently ambiguous idea in the interest of shaping engaged moral agents'.

This summary can scarcely do justice to these issues, which although on the face of it are remote from life in classrooms, in fact have everything to do with how knowledge is to be selected and used as the basis of pupil experience. My own view is that this reinterpretation of liberal education must be the central curriculum task if we are to offer all our pupils an education which gives them autonomy – the ability to solve new problems – and the capacity to marry thought and action.

19 This line of criticism is taken from Dearden (1981), where these weaknesses of the HMI argument are more extensively discussed.
20 For a fuller discussion, see W. Reid (1978).
21 A convenient commentary on the HMI primary survey is the collection of views in Richards (ed.) 1980.
22 The full survey will be found in Ashton (1981).
23 An account of this study is given in Galton, Simon, and Croll (1980).
24 This line of criticism has been taken from Garland (1979), where it is treated much more fully.
25 A critique of performance testing and the concept of assessment as a detached component of the teaching activity will be found in Holt (1981).
26 These criticisms are presented fully and cogently in Kelly (1981).
27 There is a discussion of division of responsibility between teachers and heads in middle schools in Paisey (1981).
28 This critical approach to 'skills' is a summary of the argument given by Dearden in his contribution to Richards (1980).
29 Major questions are involved. In his presidential address to the Society of Education Officers in 1978, Dudley Fiske (chief education officer for Manchester) observed:

> If we now judge that forces outside the education system require that the partnership enshrined in the 1944 Act will no longer suffice and power at the centre needs to be strengthened, we must beware of a hasty response for there are fundamental issues to debate. . . . Sometimes it seems to me that people are talking about more power for the two extremes of the three-tiered arrangement – for the Secretary of State and the schools.

During 1982, the DES is giving consideration to proposals which would modify the payment of block grants to local education authorities and have the effect of reducing their authority over education spending. At the same time, it is evident that some authorities have cut back their spending on education to unacceptable levels. There are important matters to discuss here which will not yield either to greater central control on the one hand or to cries for decentralisation on the other. It may well be that new structures for the devolution of authority will eventually be necessary.

30 An entertaining and illuminating account of management theories and their inadequacies will be found in Handy (1979). The equivalent in industrial organisations of this technocratic model of educational change is what Handy terms the 'role culture' of Apollo – the god of order and rules: 'This culture assumes that man is rational and that everything can and should be analysed in a logical fashion. . . . The Apollo style is excellent when it can be assumed that tomorrow will be like yesterday. . . . *Stability* and *predictability* are assumed and

encouraged.' It is evident that the model will appeal to bureaucratic systems like the DES, HMI and local authority management, where stability and predictability are great virtues. Unfortunately, they have little to do with the tasks of curriculum innovation, where the best decision is not obvious and outcomes are unpredictable.

31 The evidence of the HMI report *The Effects of Local Authority Expenditure on the Education Services in England* – 1981 (1982, HMSO) shows not only a serious decline in funding, but stark variations in funding levels with some LEAs making the most ruthless and debilitating cuts. In general, 'In only five LEAs were the levels of provision in the schools described as satisfactory or better under every one of the major resource headings.' Unfortunately, the political impact of this damning document was blunted by the 1982 Falklands crisis.

32 It does not, of course, follow that the solution is to remove the local jurisdiction of LEAs and allocate resources nationally. Centralised systems – like that in France – are tending to move more authority to the periphery, and the same tendency can be seen in business management. But localism always runs the risk of leading to parochialism, and this risk is greater since the 1974 local government reorganisation, which politicised educational policy-making and placed it under corporate control. There is, therefore, a case for looking again at how educational decisions are taken by LEAs, and at alternative ways of mediating authority and distributing finance. Any future administration with a genuine commitment to more just provision in national terms – and to real investment in in-service training for teachers – would need to tackle this issue.

33 A more stringently critical view of *The School Curriculum* will be found in White *et al.* (1981). Despite its defects, I incline to think the document can be used as a basis for discussion and deliberation which – at school level – could promote whole curriculum planning.

34 The most closely argued account of the deficiencies of a needs-based approach will be found in Dearden (1968).

35 My point is not to deny for a moment the uniqueness of mathematical thought, and therefore its claim as a core curriculum element (see Holt and McIntosh, 1966) but to indicate that clarity is needed about what goes into the core. It seems likely that, in this passage, the DES sees mathematics as the key to much *scientific* 'knowledge and understanding', as indeed it is: but to stress this would be to overlook the claim of mathematics to be a form of abstract inquiry in its own right. Thankfully, the Cockcroft Report (1982) turns its back on the idea that skills should be taught for their own sake, and declares 'We can in no way support or recommend an approach of this kind.' It should also be noted that the committee's study of adults' use of mathematics showed that there was no common base of general mathematical skills which all adults needed to use.

36 This, of course, is perhaps the most serious deficiency in the

government's approach to the curriculum: it reflects the unimaginative way in which economic issues have been handled by successive administrations. Despite the references to computers and the impact of microprocessors, there is no evidence that their industrial and social consequences have been explored, nor that the implications for educational programmes – and thus for the whole thrust of the curriculum – have been appreciated. The Australian document examined in the next chapter (*Core Curriculum for Australian Schools*, Curriculum Development Centre, Canberra, 1981) does attempt to take a less parochial view and paint on a larger canvas. For a thoughtful discussion of how the post-industrial society might lead to a variety of scenarios, see Robertson (1977).

37 There are important differences in the administration of education in Scotland from that in England and Wales. A useful account will be found in Bell (1981). In particular, the Scottish Education Department dates from 1872, and has an internal structure and centralised powers much closer to what exists in France than in Elizabeth House. The inspectorate in Scotland are seen as the prime agents in promoting curriculum development. It is interesting to wonder whether, because of their inherently stronger position, the Scottish inspectorate could more confidently involve outsiders in their curriculum discussions than their English colleagues. It is certainly conceivable that the final, rather conservative form of the Munn Report reflected the influence of HMI.

38 A further discussion of the Munn Report and of *Curriculum 11–16* will be found in Holt (1979).

39 A summary of recent research into the work of advisers, and of related issues in developing support agencies for curriculum change, will be found in Holt (1980).

2 Strategies and structures: approaches to curriculum change

1 An interesting account of curriculum affairs in a secondary school is given in the case study by Weston (1979).

2 The *Early Leaving* Report (Central Advisory Council for Education (England), 1954) had already indicated the cost – the educational opportunities missed – as a result of a grammar school curriculum aimed at a small elite. Lacey's case study (1970) later showed the mechanism by which such a curriculum alienated so many able pupils.

3 Moral issues of this kind, and the aim of personal autonomy, are argued in a paper by Cornall (1981) written from the point of view of a comprehensive school head.

4 There is a helpful discussion of this point in Elliott and Pring (1975).

5 An authoritative treatment of this central issue will be found in W. Reid (1978). An outline is given in Chapter 1.

6 For an extended discussion of this argument, see Sockett (1976).
7 An admirable summary of the case against behavioural objectives is given by Macdonald-Ross (1975).
8 This important matter can only be briefly treated here. The full argument will be found in Oakeshott (1962).
9 A full discussion of this point is given in Holt (1981).
10 Joseph Schwab's writings on education and curriculum are to be recommended. W. Reid (1981a) summarises the key points in Schwab's position which are relevant to whole curriculum planning. For the interested reader, Schwab's collected essays will be found in Schwab (1978).
11 For a fuller discussion, see W. Reid and Walker (1975), and W. Reid (1978).
12 These issues in whole curriculum planning are treated at length in Holt (1978).
13 See, for example, Wilcox and Eustace (1980).
14 This interesting document makes a sharp contrast with the amateurish efforts of DES and HMI in core curriculum discussion. It has aroused considerable interest in Australia and in the UK. The May 1981 issue of the Australian journal *Curriculum Perspectives* deals specifically with core curriculum, and the UK's *Journal of Curriculum Studies* regularly offers valuable comment on these matters.
15 An account of these interesting developments is given by Mavrogenes (1981).
16 In Skilbeck (1980).
17 In practice, when Re is timetabled as a separate item it tends to include Me, some Se and even some He – presumably because isolated, single periods of undiluted Re are not easily taught. But Me, at least, might be better taught in other ways than in association with Re: it can be argued that not to distinguish clearly between religious and moral issues is always objectionable, and particularly in an educational setting. To a large extent, Me will be 'caught' from school practice – from its ethos and the way staff relate with each other and with pupils. But there may be a case for using 'sensitivity material', of the kind produced by the Schools Council Moral Education Project, in an appropriate curriculum setting. Holt (1978) describes such approaches in conjunction with an expressive arts faculty linking English, music and drama.
18 For an account of American disappointments, see Grubb and Lazerson (1981). A further indication of such utilitarian developments in the UK is the decision by the DES in 1981 to suspend recognition of the Certificate of Extended Education (CEE) in favour of a post-16 examination similar to that proposed originally for one-year students in further education and outlined in *A Basis for Choice* (published in 1979 by the Further Education Curriculum Review and Development Unit within the DES). This 'pre-voc' examination has the merit of incorporating a substantial common core course, but is unfortunately

committed to behavioural objectives and student profiles. On balance, it is a sounder proposition than the CEE, which is another single-subject examination and so guarantees no core coverage. But the 'pre-voc' proposal could have a stultifying effect not only post-16, but also pre-16, where it will give a boost both to profile devices and to those who wish to make the 14–16 years more vocational in emphasis.

19 An important critique of the Bullock Report is given in Williams (1977).

20 The 1979 publication of the Association for Science Education, *Alternatives for Science Education*, gives a valuable discussion of these matters and makes important proposals. In 1981, the Schools Council has funded a major project to establish new secondary schemes in unified science.

21 The paper by Dearden will be found in Richards (ed.) (1980).

22 The importance of climate within communities – and also the latent potential a favourable climate can release in people – is emphasised in the context of industrial organisations by Townsend (1970).

23 In Popper (1976).

24 A further discussion is given in Holt (1981).

25 An account of such an assessment scheme in a comprehensive school operating a common 11–16 curriculum is given in Holt (1978).

26 The materials produced by the Avon Resources for Learning Unit, Avon LEA, Bristol are likely to be of interest to any school planning a common curriculum.

27 There is an extensive literature on MAT, but only limited take up of MAT in schools. References which can be recommended are Kelly (1978), Wragg (1976), Davies (1975), and M. Reid (1977). The Schools Council's 1977 publication *Mixed Ability Teaching in Mathematics* (Evans/Methuen) is noteworthy, and the education magazine *Forum* regularly discusses MAT. The issues of Spring 1978 and 1979 may be commended.

28 The emphasis on measurable outcomes as the basis for comparison is, for example, a serious flaw – as W. Reid (1979) has pointed out – in the 'Banbury Enquiry' (Newbold, 1977). Until recently, NFER research has been confined to this psychometric model and suffers from its limitations. But in the latest NFER investigation an interpretive style is in evidence. There is, therefore, a welcome emphasis on studying the process of MAT in M. Reid *et al.* (1981). This book can be recommended as a useful guide to the way teachers in practice make MAT work, and to the benefits they gain from it. Among its conclusions are that the more teachers use MAT, the easier they find it: and that they see its two chief benefits as the avoidance of labelling children, and the fostering of personal and social development. The HMI dislike of MAT, while embracing PSM, is thus a choice irony.

29 This concept is discussed in detail in Holt (1978).

30 A revealing account of the 'human potential' movement in the US is

given in Clare and Thompson (1981). Not the least disturbing aspect
of these developments is their anti-intellectual nature. The influence
of the mind is rejected: what matters is doing what you feel. Apart
from the obvious inconsistency (the mind decides what you feel like
doing), there is the suggestion that self-knowledge can be secured by
taking these short cuts to happiness.

31 An interesting example of such a method – in this case, the use of a
game to promote historical understanding – is given by Barker (1981).

32 Bantock's paper will be found in Golby *et al.* (1975).

33 In September 1982 two initiatives of the Manpower Services Commission threatened the notion of schooling as liberal education. The
Youth Training Scheme (YTS) is a one-year programme for all school
leavers based on the workplace. It will have a backwash effect on the
14–16 curriculum, unless its rhetoric of 'transferable skills' is resisted.
The Technical and Vocational Education Initiative (TVEI) is aimed
directly at schools and seeks to give the 14–16 curriculum a vocational
bias. It paves the way to a tripartite secondary and tertiary curriculum.
After an 11–13 banded or setted 'core' curriculum, the most able
could take a 14–18 grammar-school type course based on O and A
levels. For the below average, a 14–17 programme would combine
social and life skills with work experience and the YTS. For the
others, there would be a reincarnation of the old technical high
school: a 14–18 curriculum along TVEI lines.

These developments could sustain a divided society at a time when
the social and economic cost of such divisions is very evident. The
French – having established vocationalised post-14 schools under the
1975 Haby reforms – are now, ironically, endeavouring to devise a
more unified system. Both the YTS and the TVEI adopt a skills-based
approach assuming prespecified rules of performance, determined by
the workplace: instead of promoting the *potential* of the individual,
they imply he is *deficient* in ways which are instrumentally defined.
They are output-led (like the grammar-school model they complement), and are incompatible with a stress on process. They are
unlikely to equip our youth for a world where adaptability – the
capacity to solve new problems – will be at a premium. For they
assume that tomorrow's problems can be met by today's skills.

For a further discussion of vocationalism and the 11–16 curriculum,
see Holt, M. (1983), 'Vocationalism: the new threat to universal
education', *Forum*, May. For a penetrating discussion of the
assumptions embedded in 'social and life skills', see Elliott, J. (1983),
'A curriculum for the study of human affairs', *Journal of Curriculum
Studies*, April.

Bibliography

Ashton, P. (1981), 'Primary teachers' aims since 1969–77', in B. Simon and J. Willcocks (eds), *Research and Practice in the Primary Classroom*, Routledge & Kegan Paul.

Association for Science Education (1979), *Alternatives for Science Education*.

Barker, B. (1981), 'Ugly Ducklings', *Forum*, autumn.

Bell, R. (1981), 'Institutions of educational government', Unit 8, Course E 200, *Contemporary Issues in Education*, Open University.

Bullock Report (1975), *A Language for Life*, HMSO.

Central Advisory Council for Education (England) (1954), *Early Leaving*, HMSO.

Central Advisory Council for Education (England) (1967) *Children and their Primary Schools* (Plowden Report), HMSO.

Cheshire Education Department (1980), *Curriculum and Staffing for the 11–16 Age Range in the Secondary School* (discussion paper for working party on teacher staffing levels in secondary schools).

Clare, A. and Thompson, S. (1981), *Let's Talk About Me*, BBC Publications.

Cockcroft Report (1982), *Mathematics Counts: Report of the Committee of Inquiry into the Teaching of Mathematics in Schools*, HMSO.

Cornall, P. (1981), 'Curriculum, timetable and moral judgments', *New Universities Quarterly*, spring.

Curriculum Development Centre (1980), *Core Curriculum for Australian Schools*, Canberra.

Davies R. (1975), *Mixed Ability Teaching*, Temple Smith.

Dearden, R. (1968), *An Introduction to Primary Education*, Routledge & Kegan Paul.

Dearden R. (1981), 'Balance and coherence: some curricular principles in recent reports', *Cambridge Journal of Education*, Easter.

Department of Education and Science (DES), (1977) *Curriculum 11–16*, HMI, DES.

Bibliography

DES (1977), *Education in Schools: a Consultative Document*, DES, HMSO.

DES (1978), *Primary Education in England*, HMI, HMSO.

DES (1979), *Local Authority Arrangements for the School Curriculum*, DES, HMSO.

DES (1979), *Aspects of Secondary Education*, HMI, HMSO.

DES (1980), *A Framework for the School Curriculum*, DES, HMSO.

DES (1980), *A View of the Curriculum*, HMI, HMSO.

DES (1981), *The School Curriculum*, DES, HMSO.

DES (1981), *Curriculum 11–16: a Review of Progress*, HMI, HMSO.

DES (1982), *The Effects of Local Authority Expenditure on the Education Services in England – 1981*, HMI, HMSO.

Elliott, J., and Pring, R. (1975), *Social Education and Social Understanding*, Hodder & Stoughton.

Eustace, P., and Wilcox, B. (1977), *Curriculum Notation*, City of Sheffield Education Department.

Eustace, P., and Wilcox, B. (1980), *Tooling Up for Curriculum Review.*, NFER.

Further Education Curriculum Review and Development Unit (FEU) (1979), *A Basis for Choice*, FEU.

Galton, M., Simon, B., and Croll, P. (1980), *Inside the Primary Classroom*, Routledge & Kegan Paul.

Garland, R. (1979), 'The primary school survey: context, recommendation and implication', *Proceedings of the Exeter Society for Curriculum Studies*, June.

Golby, M. (1980), *Perspectives 2: The Core Curriculum*, Exeter University School of Education.

Golby, M. (1981), 'Practice and theory', in Lawn, M. and Barton, L. (eds), *Rethinking Curriculum Studies*, Croom Helm.

Golby M., and Lawton, D. (1981) 'What should we teach in school?' Units 28–30 of *Practical Inquiry* 2, Course U 202 Inquiry Open University.

Grubb, W.N., and Lazerson, M. (1981), 'Vocational solutions to youth problems: the persistent frustrations of the American experience', *Educational Analysis*, no. 2.

Handy, C. (1979), *Gods of Management*, Pan Books.

Hargreaves, D. (1982), *The Challenge for the Comprehensive School*, Routledge & Kegan Paul.

Hirst, P.H. (1965), 'Liberal education and the nature of knowledge', in R. Archambault (ed), *Philosophical Analysis and Education*, Routledge & Kegan Paul.

Hirst, P.H. (1967), 'The curriculum', in *Working Paper* 12, Schools Council, HMSO.

Hirst, P.H. (1982), 'Philosophy of education: the significance of the sixties', *Educational Analysis*, vol. 4, no. 1.

Holt, M. (1978), *The Common Curriculum*, Routledge & Kegan Paul.

Holt, M. (1979), *Regenerating the Curriculum*, Routledge & Kegan Paul.

Holt, M. (1980), *Schools and Curriculum Change*, McGraw-Hill.
Holt, M. (1981), *Evaluating the Evaluators*, Hodder & Stoughton.
Holt, M. and McIntosh, A. (1966), *The Scope of Mathematics*, Clarendon Press.
Hurman, A. (1978), *A Charter for Choice*, NFER.
Inner London Education Authority (ILEA) (1979), *Displaying the Curriculum*, ILEA.
Inner London Education Authority (ILEA) (1981), *ILEA Statement on the Curriculum for Pupils Aged 5 to 16*, March, ILEA.
Kelly, A.V. (1978), *Mixed Ability Grouping*, Harper & Row.
Kelly, A.V. (1981), 'Research and the primary classroom', *Journal of Curriculum Studies*, no. 3.
Lacey, C. (1970), *Hightown Grammar*, Manchester University Press.
Lawton, D. (1973), *Social Change, Education Theory and Curriculum Planning*, Hodder & Stoughton.
Lawton, D. (1980), *The Politics of the School Curriculum*, Routledge & Kegan Paul.
Macdonald-Ross, M. (1975), 'Behavioural objectives: a critical review', in M. Golby *et al.* (eds) (1976), *Curriculum Design*, Croom Helm.
Manpower Services Commission (1981), *Skills for Working Life*, report of national conference, Stoke Rochford Hall, June.
Mavrogenes, N. (1981), 'Latin in the elementary school: a help for reading and language arts', *Latin Teaching*, No. 1.
Neal, D. (1982), 'Spirituality across the Curriculum', mimeo, College of St Mark and St John, Plymouth.
Newbold, D. (1977), *Ability Grouping: the Banbury Enquiry*, NFER.
Nottinghamshire Education Department (1980), *The Staffing of Secondary Schools*, report of education sub-committee.
Oakeshott, M. (1962), *Rationalism in Politics*, Methuen.
OECD (1976), 'Report on Britain', *The Times Higher Education Supplement*, 9 May.
Paisey, A. (1981), *Small Organisations: the Management of Primary and Middle Schools*, NFER-Nelson.
Phenix, P. (1964), *Realms of Meaning*, McGraw-Hill.
Popper, K. (1976), *Unended Quest: an Intellectual Autobiography*, Fontana.
Reid, M. (1977), 'Mixed feelings', *The Times Educational Supplement*, 10 June.
Reid, M., Clunies-Ross, L., Goacher, B., and Vile, C. (1981), *Mixed Ability Teaching: Problems and Possibilities*, NFER-Nelson.
Reid, W. (1978), *Thinking About the Curriculum*, Routledge & Kegan Paul.
Reid, W. (1979), 'Making the problem fit the method', *Journal of Curriculum Studies* no. 2.
Reid, W. (1980), 'Democracy, perfectability and the battle of the books; thoughts on the conception of liberal education in the writings of Schwab', *Curriculum Inquiry*, vol. 10, no. 3.

Bibliography

Reid, W. (1981a), 'Curriculum design and moral judgment', paper presented at conference 'The Whole Curriculum: Problems and Possibilities', Cambridge Institute of Education, September.

Reid, W. (1981b), 'The deliberative approach to the study of the curriculum and its relation to critical pluralism', in Lawn, M., and Barton, L. (eds), *Rethinking Curriculum Studies*, Croom Helm.

Reid. W. and Walker, D. (1975), *Case Studies in Curriculum Change*, Routledge & Kegan Paul.

Reynolds, J. and Skilbeck, M. (1976), *Culture and the Classroom*, Open Books.

Richards, C. (ed) (1980), *The Primary Curriculum: Issues for the Eighties*, A. and C. Black.

Robertson, J. (1977), 'Towards post-industrial liberation and reconstruction', *New Universities Quarterly*, winter.

Schools Council (1967), *The Educational Implications of Social and Economic Change*, Working Paper 12, HMSO.

Schools Council (1971), *Choosing a Curriculum for the Young School Leaver*, Working Paper 33, Evans/Methuen.

Schools Council (1977), *Mixed Ability Teaching in Mathematics*, Evans/Methuen.

Schools Council (1981), *The Practical Curriculum*, Evans/Methuen.

Schwab, J. (1963), *The Teaching of Science as Enquiry*, Harvard University Press.

Schwab, J. (1969), 'The practical: a language for curriculum', *School Review*, November.

Schwab, J. (1978), *Science, Curriculum, and Liberal Education*, selected essays edited by I. Westbury and N. Wilkof, University of Chicago Press.

Scottish Education Department (1977) *The Structure of the Curriculum in the Third and Fourth Years of the Scottish Secondary School* (Munn Report), HMSO.

Skilbeck, M. (1976) 'Forms and fields: a knowledge-based curriculum', Unit 4, Course E 203, *Curriculum Design and Development*, Open University.

Skilbeck, M. (1980), 'Core curriculum and the role of the school in curriculum development', *Monash Education Public Lectures: Education in the 80s*, Curriculum Development Centre, Canberra.

Sockett, H. (1976), 'Aims and objectives', Unit 12, Course E 203, *Curriculum Design and Development*, Open University.

Stenhouse, L. (1975), *An Introduction to Curriculum Development*, Heinemann.

Townsend, R. (1970), *Up the Organisation*, Michael Joseph.

Warnock Report, (1978), *Special Educational Needs*, HMSO.

Weston, P. (1979), *Negotiating the Curriculum*, NFER.

White, J. (1973), *Towards a Compulsory Curriculum*, Routledge & Kegan Paul.

White, J. *et al.* (1981), *No Minister: A Critique of the DES Paper 'The School Curriculum'*, University of London Institute of Education.
Williams, J. (1977), *Learning to Write, or Writing to Learn?* NFER.
Williams, R. (1961), *The Long Revolution*, Chatto & Windus.
Wragg, E. (ed) (1976), *Teaching Mixed Ability Groups*, David & Charles.
Wilcox, B., and Eustace, P. (1980), *Tooling Up for Curriculum Review*, NFER.

Index

192